KNUCKLE

KNUCKLE

JAMES QUINN McDONAGH

HarperElement
An imprint of HarperCollins*Publishers*
1 London Bridge Street
London SE1 9GF

First published by Collins 2012
This edition 2015

www.harpercollins.co.uk

1

A catalogue record for this book is
available from the British Library.

ISBN 978-0-00-746703-7

I would like to dedicate this book to my grandson,
James Quinn McDonagh

CONTENTS

Prologue

ANY EDGE IS WORTH HAVING

It was half-six in the morning when my eyes flicked open. Normally I would have been up half an hour already, into my clothes and out for a run. But with today being the day of the fight I wasn't moving. All the exhausting weeks of training were now over – whatever else happened today, that was done with. An end to the jogging, weight-lifting, circuit training, the sparring that had gone on day after day for three months.

The last couple of weeks I had been winding down my training anyway, as I didn't want to risk an injury in the days before the fight, but it was still a relief to think it was over. No more hitting bags for over an hour at a time. I could sleep a bit longer, I could eat what I wanted, and, what was more important, I could go out and enjoy myself again. I could drink what I wanted, when I wanted. No more sneaking out on a Sunday night to sink a few pints. No more setting out to jog on a Monday morning with a hangover, and turning up at the gym dripping wet – having cheated by getting a lift most of the way and pouring some water over my head just before I got there to make it look like I'd been sweating with the effort I'd put in.

Was I ready? I didn't know. I'd done everything I could to be ready, but it was never easy. I was probably in the best shape I had ever been in. I had trained more intensively for this fight than any I had fought before. I was physically at my best and I knew that; I felt confident. I had my plans – I'd thought long and hard about how to fight, how I was going to act, and how I was going to beat him. I'd thought of what I might have to do if that didn't work, so I had my back-up plan as well. I was prepared.

No one, though, is ever really ready for a fight like this. A man could go out and get a punch to the head that could kill him. Or he could kill someone. If I hit the man hard, like I planned to, but he slipped and fell, banged his head down on the ground – he could die. That would be with me for ever.

I lay in bed and said a few prayers. I blessed myself and prayed to God for my health, that of my wife and boys, and of my family. I said the Our Father and the Hail Mary. I prayed that the fight would go well, and that I would win. I guessed that I wasn't the only one praying that day to win my fight but I thought, Lord, I didn't ask for this fight, he did, so listen to me first.

ANY EDGE IS WORTH HAVING

You've got to try. Any edge is worth having.

Theresa stirred beside me and I said, 'I'm going to go and get some milk and the papers,' and got up and dressed. We were living in a settled house then, in a quiet area of Dundalk, in County Louth, and the shops were close by. Back home again, I started reading the papers over a cup of tea. I wasn't trying to distract myself; I was calm, and relaxed. I knew I'd done everything I could to prepare for today and just had to wait till it was time to leave for the fight.

When a fight is called, each side will appoint their own referee from a neutral clan. It's up to the two referees to see that fair play takes place, but before they start, the arrangements for the fight itself have to be sorted out. Both sides have to agree to the site of the fight, and the timing. Sometimes this can drag on, and then I'd know that the other side was messing with my head to get their edge over me.

I was going to be fighting Paddy Joyce – 'the Lurcher', he'd been nicknamed – around lunchtime. That was the idea anyway. The fight could have been delayed, though, so I needed to eat a meal that would last me through the day; I couldn't be doing with getting hungry or tired at the wrong time. So instead of my usual breakfast I needed to get a decent meal in me now as it would most likely be the only food I'd get till the evening. I had put aside a sirloin steak in the fridge for the morning, along with some onions and a couple of eggs. That did fine.

About 9 a.m. my daddy, Jimmy Quinn, and my brothers Curly Paddy, Michael and Dave showed up. We had a cup of tea together, the four of them offering me encouragement all the time. Curly Paddy and Michael had been some of my sparring partners and they kept me focused on what I had to do later on. JJ, my son, had kept me company while I trained, and now he sat quietly with his uncles and Auld Jimmy while we talked. All the time, my phone didn't stop ringing, people telling me they were coming down to support me, calling to wish me success, that sort of thing. I decided to make my way over to my uncle Thomas's as I didn't want the rest of the clan turning up on my doorstep. My neighbours had already complained about the number of cars parked around my home, some blocking their driveways, and my landlady had made it clear she didn't much care for travellers. A hundred or so milling about outside my front door wouldn't make me a popular man, but at my uncle Thomas's site no one would care. Thomas didn't really go in for the fighting himself, but he was happy to have us gather there and to see me off when it was time.

When I was ready to go I took Theresa to one side, told her I was going to win my fight, and promised to come back safely. 'God bless you, James,' she said, though she wasn't happy I was fighting. She wanted me to win – 'Up the Quinn McDonaghs!' she'd say when I went off – but she wasn't happy; she never had been. All the time I'd been training she'd been the one holding the family together; she always held the family together. 'Take this and keep it with you,' she said, and pressed into my hand a small laminated picture of a saint. Whenever I fought I'd receive these little gifts from the women in the family, my mother and aunts included. As I fought with no vest on I only had one place to slip these relics, as we called them, into, and that was my sock. By the time I left for my uncle's site, I had five of them to fit in.

When we reached the site the clan had already started gathering. The Quinn McDonaghs all lived close by, our name marking out the triangle of land we thought of as home: from Dublin out west to Mullingar, up north to Dundalk and back south to Dublin again. There are Sligo McDonaghs, Mohan McDonaghs, Bumby McDonaghs, Galway McDonaghs, Mayo McDonaghs, even McDonaghs in England; but the Quinn McDonaghs are confined to that triangle of near enough fifty miles by fifty miles by fifty miles. At my uncle Thomas's site, my uncles and cousins – dozens of them – were standing about waiting. One wore a white T-shirt printed with:

James
The Mightey
Quinn
Mc
Donagh

To pass the time they were playing a game of toss. I joined in, just to keep myself busy more than anything else. Heads and harps, we used to call it before the Euro came in. When I was 12 years old I'd see men out in Cara Park, in Dublin, tossing coins on a Thursday, when 'the labour' paid out in the morning. They'd lose all the money they'd just been given to feed their families for the rest of the week: forty, fifty pounds gone, just on the chance that the coin would keep coming up heads. They'd have three or four small kids and they'd have to go back to their wives and family with their dole gone, lost in the toss pit. They'd struggle on for the following week, and then go straight out to gamble again.

If the coin turned up harps, then the other guy would step in. I've seen men walk away from the toss pit with up to IR£800 in their hands. I've lost six hundred in an afternoon myself, all on the toss of a coin. I had a run of luck that day that didn't help. It was at my brother Michael's wedding, and I had to borrow two hundred from someone else just to have some spending money for the rest of the evening. I felt bad about that but it helped me when it came to a fight – I knew what it was like to lose money, and didn't want to lose the purse. I knew how bad I felt after losing a few hundred, so how bad would it be if I was to lose ten, twenty, or even thirty grand?

I won a little bit and lost a little bit of money that day at the wedding. I didn't take that as any kind of omen at all – it was just something that relaxed me. Playing toss meant I didn't go into fight mode too early. Trying to get myself up too soon would just make me tense and tired. It was only when I was on my way to the fight that I'd get into character. That may sound funny, but it's true. I'm not a violent man; to take up the challenge of these fights was something I did for our family name. The character the rival clans – the Joyces, the Nevins – thought I was, some kind of tough guy – they'd created that. I hadn't. I had no interest in fighting other than defending the name of the Quinn McDonaghs, and winning that purse.

Soon there were well over a hundred people around me. The Quinn McDonaghs were out in force because I was fighting for our name and they'd come to support me. My uncle Chappy – one of the nicest people I know – came over, and he was riled up by the fight. He gripped my arm with his hand. 'James, you listen to me. You see them people' – he waved south, in the direction of where the fight would take place, and I nodded as he continued – 'all them Joyces and all them Nevins. They've never beaten you. Now you've done your training, you know what you're doing. Come back here and do not lose. I'm telling you straight: do not lose this, you make sure that you beat him, and if you beat him you've them all beat.' That's how much it meant to everyone, that even someone like Chappy could get worked up by the fight. If I beat the Lurcher, then, as Chappy told me, 'That's them people gone

9

for ever.' Big Joe Joyce had said the same to me when he called to arrange the day and time of the fight. 'You're fighting the best man of the Joyces. If you beat him, there'll be no more. We'll leave you alone,' he'd said, although I didn't think for a moment they would. The only hope I had of making sure they didn't send for me again was if I really hurt the Lurcher. That might be the only way of stopping further fights.

I knew, too, what it would mean if I lost this fight. Then every Joyce and Nevin would be queuing up to take a shot at the Quinn McDonaghs. The other clans had pushed me up onto this place where I was their target, so if one of them managed to knock me down, then in their eyes they would have knocked down the whole Quinn McDonagh clan. To them that's what this fight meant.

A reporter had shown up who'd heard about the fight and wanted to come and talk to me and then put some pictures of the fight in the paper. I told him why we were fighting. 'There's bad blood between the two families, and it's been going on for years.' My dad added, 'Fifty years.' The reporter also asked about the purse and if the fight was really about that. I smiled but explained that all that meant was 'a few quid for Christmas too'.

What the reporter didn't understand was that if I did win, I wasn't winning £20,000. When we got the money at the end of the fight we'd first give each referee £500. And then I hadn't put up £10,000 on my own; my family and I had gone to uncles and cousins and everyone would put in a little, a few hundred or maybe more. That way, if I lost, no one lost a lot of money, and if I won, then everyone would get a little share. Winning the fight wouldn't make me a rich man, but I didn't tell the reporter that.

The rest of my cousins and uncles then came over to offer me a few words of praise, encouragement and advice. Back-seat drivers, I call them; people with great beer guts who lived in the pub and had never trained in their lives telling me what to do, how to put myself about – and I was the one who'd put in about fourteen weeks' training for this. So I smiled and thanked them but I didn't really listen. Once I was standing there in front of Paddy the Lurcher, I'd be the only one who was there to fight him.

I didn't know what sort of fighter he was going to be, because I'd never seen him fight, although he would have seen the videos of my fights. I didn't even know what he looked like now, as I hadn't seen him since the London days nearly four-teen years ago. I'd had some feedback from someone who'd seen him train, and the report said he'd bust the punch-bag hanging in Big Joe's shed during training.

Hang on a second; how can you bust a punch-bag? Muhammad Ali didn't bust a punch-bag. What bag was the Lurcher boxing now? A paper bag? A plastic bag? The man is an animal, I was told. He's breaking the bags off the wall. You're better off calling the fight off. Was this a game plan of the Joyces? I wondered. There was an awful lot of money riding on this fight and if I refused to fight him I'd lose it all. Was I being fed some line here? Was this meant to get back to me to upset me in my training?

That wasn't for me to worry about; if anything, it inspired me to train harder. I kept a clear head; I'd fought before, and each time the fight had been out in the open air. This man hadn't, and his record was one of bullying people, and all the tales I'd heard – of him beating this man, beating that – didn't worry me because I had no way of knowing if they were people he knew he could beat before a fight, if they were no match for him. There were no tapes to watch, so they could have been what we call 'fair fights', or they might not have been. I wasn't going to give him a chance, and I figured that if I kept my concentration, stuck to my plans, changed from one plan to another if necessary when I was fighting, I'd be OK. I knew I was fit enough.

When I was a kid growing up, I'd trained to be a boxer, I'd learned the basic moves. Left hand slightly out, right hand just above the chin, left leg out, back leg secure. From the age of 16, though, I had no training and the moves that I'd learned before I'd now refined into my own style. Come out, step forward, hit, step off. I'd sparred with people the Lurcher's size, as far as I could tell, and I'd prepared myself to move quickly so he wouldn't be able use his height and weight against me.

While I was fighting I'd keep my left arm out in front of me, feeling my way, my fist close to whoever I was fighting so my opponent couldn't see me clearly enough. If he tried to slap my left arm away, the next minute my right would be sitting in his face. 'The fishing pole', the Joyces and the Nevins called it. They didn't like it one bit. It disturbed my opponents, and broke their concentration. All my trainers when I was in boxing clubs as a young teenager told me not to use my left arm like that, but it was a tactic that always worked for me. I wasn't going to change it, because it kept me at arm's length from danger, I'd tell everyone. It was a shield to protect me. I could use it like a poker, jabbing at someone's eye.

Ned Stokes, my referee, and two of his sons drove into the site about half-eleven. We shook hands. 'I wish you luck, James. I hope it goes well for you,' he said. I took a phone call off Paddy's referee, Patrick McGinley, and relayed what he'd said to me to Ned: that we were meeting him and the Lurcher in a place down in Drogheda, about twenty miles to the south. To the cheers and applause of the waiting crowd, we got into Ned's car, his sons in the one behind, and drove away.

From Dundalk it was just under half an hour's drive on the M1. As he drove Ned Stokes talked about nothing in particular, a pleasant chat designed to take my mind off what the next couple of hours would bring. Once we came off the motorway and into Drogheda I had to find somewhere to wind myself up and get myself into fight mode. My phone would still have been ringing if I hadn't switched it off. Having a moment to yourself is a rare thing for any traveller, and as for myself I found that there were some days when my house felt like Piccadilly Circus. I needed some time alone now. 'Pull into this McDonald's, will you, Ned,' I said. 'I need to use the toilet.'

Above the washbasins in the toilet was a mirror. I stared into it and spoke to myself. 'This is your day, pal. Are you going to do it?' I hadn't planned to talk to myself, it just came to me at that moment. I thought of what those lads, my supporters, had been telling me to do; good things, advising me, encouraging me, telling me that the Lurcher was no good and that he couldn't fight, and trying to get me worked up. But they weren't here now, I told myself. I was the one who'd have to go out and fight for them all, for the Quinn McDonagh name. The weight of that lay heavily on my shoulders and on some days that pressure told on me, but today wasn't one of those days. I was strong and fit and determined, and I wanted to go and fight Paddy. I wanted to hit him, to hurt him. To do that now meant I had to hate him. I remembered seeing him in London years ago, watching him bully people, and I focused on that as it helped me create that hatred. This was part of what I had to do – slipping into the role of James the fighter, James Quinn, son of Jimmy Quinn, a role I only have because it's been forced on me.

It wasn't hard to find reasons to hate Paddy Lurch; for the past few months I'd neglected so much of my life as

I concentrated on this fight, what with the training and the dieting. If I didn't work, I didn't earn any money. I'd not spent time with my family. Instead I'd been in the gym, in that boxing ring, day after day for weeks on end. I'd not been to the pub to enjoy myself. I'd had to stop almost everything I was doing so that I could be ready for today. Paddy was the cause of that and the more I thought about what I'd had to stop and what I'd missed out on, the angrier I became. I wanted him to feel the pain that I'd felt for those endless weeks, the pain I'd felt in my muscles and joints as I trained, the aches I'd had those early mornings as I pulled myself out of bed to go jogging. I'd used every moment of the last few weeks to focus my anger on him. No spare time, no drink. No work, no money. All because of the Lurcher.

I needed to get angry because I had to stand in front of Paddy and try to hurt him. I had to be ready to cut his face, to cause him to get stitches under his eyes. Ready to knock him down, ready to give him concussion. Ready to disfigure him with a blow to the nose or the cheek. Ready to hit him hard enough on the head to give him a haemorrhage. Did I care? No. I hadn't asked for this fight. He had. He was the one who'd made us do this, not me, and I used that to get myself more angry, to really start to hate the man and all those in his clan who'd put him up to fight me. We were here because of him, we were both risking our health and maybe even our lives because of him, and that made me angrier still.

A travelling man's life is shorter than a settled man's; the average life expectancy for a travelling man is sixty-seven years. That's twenty years less than for a settled man. We Quinn McDonaghs have a high rate of heart disease and cancer; there's heart problems in many of my uncles as well as my mother and father. So why was I adding to the problem by going out to maybe end this man's life or maybe – if I took a blow in a bad way – my own? The anger boiled hotter.

Good. It was working. I looked into the mirror and repeated, 'Today, James, you can do it.'

I had been provoked into this fight, and I had no choice but to win it. I had to succeed because if I didn't hit him, hurt him, knock him down and keep him there, he'd do exactly that to me. I didn't want to do this. I'm not someone who seeks fights; I've never looked for a scuffle in a pub on a Saturday night. I wasn't proud that I was going to be doing this, I wasn't happy; but this is what the fights were about. If I was going to win it was because I was ready to do everything I had to. I hated the Lurcher with a vengeance. I had to, otherwise I wasn't going to win my fight. If I hadn't hated him, I'd have felt sorry for him, I'd have felt pity – but I didn't. I didn't feel sorrow or pity, or compassion. I felt hatred. I wanted to get stuck in, hurt and maim that person. Hurting him badly would make another man think twice before challenging me, and that meant no more fights. So the hatred drove my aggression, and I needed that. That person has upset my whole life, I was thinking, and he's getting me a name that I don't like.

The name. It was all about the name.

I left the toilet and got back into the front car. While I'd been inside, Ned had taken the call telling us which location to go to, so with one of his sons in the car behind we set off again. The location was only five minutes away. I held my hands out to the lads in the back and they went to work, running bandages over my hands, thumbs and wrists.

As soon as we arrived at the site I wasn't happy. I climbed out of the car and looked around but I knew we weren't going to stay. There was nothing wrong with the place itself; it was the number of people already there to watch the fight I wasn't pleased to see. I had deliberately left my family behind, and nobody had come with me except the referee, who was independent anyway, and his two sons; a cameraman, to tape the fight so that it could be seen by everyone back in Dundalk later on; and my second, who I needed to tie up my bandages. I'd expected Paddy Lurch to have the same around him too. Instead there was a gang of about fifteen or so there, hanging about waiting for the fight to start. I recognised some faces right away, people I'd fought in the past, Chaps Patrick, Ditsy Nevin, and a dozen or so other Nevins hanging around with them both. There is no doubt whose side they'd all be on when the fight started and I didn't think that made it fair at all. No wonder Paddy Lurch had suggested this place for the fight. He might as well have said we'd fight at his house.

I got back into the car. 'I ain't fighting here,' I said to Ned. He said, 'Yes, the agreement we made was none of them people were coming to the fight, there was no other spectators.' Patrick McGinley had come over to talk to Ned and had his head in through the driver's window and he heard what Ned was saying. 'That's all right, James,' Patrick said. 'If you don't want to fight here, then we won't fight here.'

The Nevins didn't like it when they saw me get back into the car. Chaps Patrick, though, came up and said, 'Would you mind, James, if me and the lad come to the fight?' He had his young son with him, a boy of about 7 or 8. Why he wanted to bring a kid to watch two men knock lumps out of each other I don't know. 'That's all right, I don't mind if you two come but' – I pointed at the Nevins lined up alongside Ditsy – 'I don't want those others there.'

This set Ditsy off. Ned was turning the car round and Ditsy started yelling at me, 'Get out and fucking fight, you cowardly fuck, yer. Get out and fight yer man here.' I turned to Ned and said, 'Now you see why I don't want them there.' Ned said, 'James, I understand 100 per cent,' and we drove away, Ditsy still gesturing and yelling at the car as we left him behind.

Ned drove to the end of a quiet back lane outside Drogheda, and the car with his boys and one with Chaps Patrick followed on. The bandages on my fists were tightened and checked by my second and I pulled off my sweatshirt and started to walk back up the lane to where we were going to fight. It was a grey November day, probably cold, but I didn't notice, as I'd started to block out what was going on around me. I was narrowing my focus on the things that mattered now, because concentration would win me the fight. One moment when I was not looking at my opponent, where his fists were, what his feet were doing, and – most importantly – where his eyes were looking to, and it could all be over. I'd learned that; fighting someone, their eyes would look where they wanted to go to next, where they wanted to aim for, where they were planning to hit me. It never failed, this; I knew I had a moment to strike back before they could hit me if their eyes led the way. I never took my gaze off my opponent's face; if I had to hit him on his chin, I knew it was somewhere below his eyes and nose. I didn't need to look to know that.

At this point I still hadn't seen the Lurch. Ahead I could see a couple of cars pull up and stop, and a guy got out of one of them. I knew that Paddy was a red-haired feller, big, and I believed a little slow in his movements; but this man was rolling his shoulders, stretching out his neck, shaping himself in a way that I hadn't expected – someone who knew what he was about. I asked Ned, 'Is that Paddy Lurch? Is that the Lurch, Ned?' 'No,' he said, looking over at the man. 'That's young Maguire.' I didn't even know what the Lurch looked like and I was about to fight him.

Then he stepped out of McGinley's car and there was no doubt this was him. He was as big as me, in tracksuit bottoms and a red vest, and bandages on his hands. I nodded over and he nodded back at me, the courtesy of a head wave but no more. The two referees came over to check my bandages – to make sure I'd nothing tied under the bandages that would make a punch more painful – and were happy enough with them. Then they called the Lurcher, still wearing his red vest, over and we listened while Ned ran over the rules. 'The agreement is, if a man is down he gets up. Arms round each other is a foul, but when you're in tight, no man can stop it. No fouling, no dirty punches. If you break, you break clean.'

The Lurch pulled off his vest and said, 'There's one thing I want to say, James: your brother Paddy's the cause of all of this.'

'Lurch, there's no need for this,' I told him. 'You shouldn't have sent for me, you should have sent for Paddy.'

'I don't send for murderers,' he replied. The fight hadn't started and he was goading me. I started to answer back but Ned broke in.

'Excuse me, boys,' he said, talking over us both. 'No bad language, boys.'

'No biting, no holding, no head-butting,' added Patrick McGinley. 'Now shake hands.'

'No,' Paddy said immediately, and I retorted, 'No, no shaking hands.'

ANY EDGE IS WORTH HAVING

The referees stepped back.

I moved forward, hopping from foot to foot, my left arm in front of me, right curled back, ready to land the first blow.

1

BORN A TRAVELLER

rowing up, this fighting thing never came into my mind. I never thought either about being a policeman, being a solicitor, being a fireman – none of those. I was a traveller, and they weren't things that I would even have thought of doing with my life. I would do what travellers did. That was the only path open to me.

I was born in County Westmeath in 1967. For my first few years I lived with my grandfather, Auld Daddy, my mother, older brother Curly Paddy and older sister Bridgie, all of us in an old-fashioned barrel-top wagon, the kind pulled by horses. The main bed was inside at the back of the wagon, and there was a little stove to keep us warm and a box for the bread. To keep me safe when I was a baby while he slept, my grandfather would loop a bit of rope around my middle and tie the other end around his ankle. If I tried to crawl off, the rope would tug and he'd wake up.

Auld Daddy had two horses, one to tow the wagon, the other to breed from, so we could sell the foals. We wouldn't sleep in the wagon, not us kids anyway; we would sleep under the wagon, or at the side of the road in a 'tent' made of branches from the hedges. The dogs would sleep anywhere they could; they weren't pets, they were working dogs. My mother would cook on an open fire, and she'd wash our clothes with water from the river. In the summertime, when it was warm, we'd sit by the fire and we'd sing songs and be told stories of Irish myths from many years ago. The story-teller, usually Auld Daddy, would tell us ghost stories about the banshees, to frighten us off to bed.

We'd sleep in the tent, in straw that the farmer would give us when we arrived. My mother would shake it all up, spread the blanket out, and I'd climb in. I'd wrap the blanket round me and as I sank into the straw it would just fall around me. It was like a big quilt, nice and warm on a cold night.

To an outsider it might have looked romantic, a simple life like that, but it wasn't, it was very hard. In the summer it might have looked the same as a nice camping trip but if you go camping you only go for a few days and then come home, whereas we were living like that all year round. In the winter it was a very harsh life. Rural Ireland was poor then and travellers were the poorest of the poor. In those days travellers lived off the land, making things like clothes pegs that could be sold door to door and at the markets, and from the seasonal work farmers would give them, such as picking spuds in the autumn. We had to beg for clothes from the local families, the settled people. We had no other way of getting basics of that sort.

I was born when my father was in England. He'd travelled over there for work, got mixed up in some trouble, and ended up in prison. If years back a man was in jail or away working, his wife would go back to her family, so my mother went back to her father, and he looked after her. The first time my father saw me I was 2½ years old.

My father was Jimmy Quinn, son of Mikey Quinn. Those names go through the generations: I'm James Quinn, it's my son's name, and my grandson's name, and before Mikey came Martin, and before him was Mickey McDonagh. Mickey married a woman called Judy Caffrey and together they had five sons and five daughters. Mickey's mother was one of three sisters known as 'the Long Tails' for the dresses they wore. All these names I grew up with around the fire; there was nothing written down about our family and stories like those, about these memorable dresses, only survive because they were passed on. Travellers' lives were mostly just hidden away in history. Mickey's son Martin was my great-grandfather and he went on to have five sons as well. His wife was a Joyce, Winnie Joyce, and her brother Patsy married Martin's sister, linking the Joyces and the Quinn McDonaghs together right through to this day. One of my grandfather's brothers also had several children, among them Padnin Quinn, Davey 'Minor Charge' Quinn, and Cowboy Quinn – and my mother. The Nevins also married into the family back in those generations – so we're all related, even if we do feud with each other.

There is a Quinn connection going back a long way, even though we're the Quinn McDonaghs. I never knew why we always made such a thing of the 'Quinn' part and didn't really pay much attention to the 'McDonagh' bit, but I was told two versions of the story when I was growing up. Both involve Mickey McDonagh coming back into a camp, chased by the police. One version says it was because he was running from them after stealing something, the other says it was because he didn't want to be conscripted into the British Army for the First World War. Either way, when the police came into the camp and discovered there were five Michael McDonaghs on the site, he was asked, 'Are you Mickey McDonagh?', to which he said 'Me? No, I'm Michael Quinn,' taking his mother's maiden name (Abigail Quinn was another of the Long Tail sisters), and from then on the Quinn McDonagh name was used.

My uncle Michael was known as Chappy; my uncle Martin was known as Buck; my uncle Kieran was known as Johnny Boy. Most of the time I never knew why some people had the nicknames they had, but even as children we all knew why my father's cousin Bullstail Collins was called Bullstail and not Martin Collins. One day he was standing by a farmer's gate and the bull in the field was scratching his arse against the fence. Martin Collins decided to tie his tail onto the gate and hit him with the stick. The bull went and the tail stayed – and that's why he's always known as Bullstail.

When I was growing up my dad travelled with his family round the area of Ireland we lived in, and when I was a little boy I loved to hear their stories. My father grew up with seven brothers and five sisters, and with all those mouths to feed everyone had to contribute. (Large families were a feature of traveller life, and my sister married a man with twenty-two brothers and sisters. My own wife Theresa has seventeen uncles and aunts.) In the 1940s and 1950s life on the roads was very, very rough, and my father used to say if it hadn't been for the farmers the travelling people of Ireland wouldn't have survived. The farmers gave them work and – when they were able to – donations of food and clothing as well. My father's family lived off what they could earn and what they were given.

One of the stories we all heard when growing up was about the Christmastime when my father went out, with two of his older sisters, to see if they could get him some shoes. He was only 3½ years old. 'I was walking out with nothing on my bare feet, in the snow,' he'd say, and we'd all try to imagine how cold that must have been. His childhood had gone quickly and by the age of 11 he was in the fields with his family picking spuds from August through to the winter. 'The first day's wages I ever got,' he'd tell us as we sat by the crackling fire, 'was a half a crown for walking with a plough over at Carnaross, County Meath, and that's back in the 1950s.' He would describe his battle with the heavy plough and the thick, heavy soil. With his wages he bought a beer but he'd always make sure we knew that he'd 'given my mother a shilling'.

The family would eat what they could find, and share what they had with whoever was around them. My father loved to tell us about the time he and his brother Buck went out and gathered some spuds and carrots from the field, which they gave to their mother to put in her large pot (as children we all feared the witches' pot, as we called it). Then they went out and caught a couple of rabbits and a hare, and then managed to catch a duck in a local pond, and – and this was the risky thing – a pheasant too. All of these went into the pot with whatever else my granny could find and their family, and the five families around them, feasted on that for dinner. As children we couldn't understand how anyone could eat all of those things at one time, but I suppose if you're very hungry, as they all were, you wouldn't care. Certainly my father remembered the entire pot being emptied that night.

Just as we were told how good and kind the farmers and their families were in those days, we'd also be reminded of what could happen if we weren't respectful of them in return. When my father was young, his uncle was out in Galway somewhere and had a confrontation with the farmer beside whose land he was staying. The farmer accused him of raiding the hedges for timber to keep his fire going and my father's uncle denied this, saying he'd scavenged the timber from where it had fallen on the side of the road. He stood up to talk to the farmer, and the farmer claimed he saw him pulling out an iron bar and thought he was going to hit him, so he produced a gun and blew my dad's uncle's head off. Killed him like that, over his own fire by the side of the road. The farmer was taken to court about it but he claimed he'd shot him in self-defence and no one disagreed with him. So we were told always to mind what the farmer told us and not to think we could do as we liked. That story was often repeated to us to remind us that the law didn't always look too favourably on travellers and so we should be careful not to come into contact with the police if we could help it.

There were times when we relied on the Guards – what travellers called the Garda, the Irish Police. In my father's young days no traveller had a telephone – just as we didn't when I was young, of course – so if there was a death, or another reason to need to meet up with another family, then it was the Guards who would pass on a message. A traveller would go into the local Garda office and ask them to pass on a message to the Quinn McDonaghs up in Meath. The Garda would then ring some local stations and ask if we were known to be in the area, and if so, could an officer go out and find the family and carry a message to them? Usually the Guards would know who was in their area and roughly where they were, so it wouldn't take them long to find whoever they were looking for.

The story we liked best was the one about my father meeting my mother for the first time, in 1963. He was back in Ireland, home from work in England. In the 1950s and the early 1960s many travelling men left Ireland and went to Manchester. They had heard there was work to be had there; on the side of the roads there was work in the Irish construction companies. Names like McGinley, McAlpine, you name it, my father worked for them all. Back home on holiday, he was on a bike, heading down to the water pump, when he happened upon this girl on her way to fetch some milk. At this point in the story my mother would interrupt. There was no accident about it, she'd declare; he knew where she'd be and he'd ridden down there to the pump deliberately, in the hope of seeing her. That she was related to him made the meeting easier, as there wasn't much mixing with other clans when they travelled. People mostly stuck to themselves. It was usually only at arranged events, like the horse fairs, that boys and girls would get a chance to see each other and talk. That, and family get-togethers such as weddings.

I was born on a Tuesday in hospital and christened the following Sunday, 23 July, in the Cathedral of Christ the King in Mullingar, County Westmeath. (Years later I was married there.) My father was by then in prison in England – there was a stabbing incident in a pub and he was put inside for three years – and I was brought up by my mother and my grandfather. My mother told me many years later that she found it hard going, raising the three of us boys without her husband there. She'd go door to door looking for hand-me-downs, trying to make the money she had been given last a week. The relieving officer would give her money or sometimes a voucher to exchange for food. His title was shortened to 'leaving officer' and the one I can remember my mother mentioning was called Mr Scally. He was nice to us and if we were out on the road he'd come past in his car, pull over, and come out with the money or the voucher for us. No more than four or five pounds, it wasn't much, but it helped.

Eventually my father was released and he came straight over to see us. Well, not exactly straight; he went to meet my mother's brother to find where we were and the two of them – drinking companions from their young days – went out to celebrate his release that night. This is what travelling men do, so I suppose it's no surprise that the following morning they did it all over again, and it wasn't until much later that day that my father finally laid eyes on the son he'd not yet seen.

'What do you remember about seeing me for the first time, Daddy?' I asked my father once. He thought for a moment or two. 'You was in bed, and you were a big lump of a boy,' he said, which wasn't exactly the touching memory I'd hoped to hear.

KNUCKLE

The very next morning my father saddled up the horses, which up until then my mother had looked after, and we set off, leaving Auld Daddy behind. There was no time to waste. Having no one he could turn to for help, my father needed to earn some money as quickly as he could. For the next few years we lived on the side of the road, although when my father first came back we moved about a fair bit. Maybe he was restless after being locked up in England, I don't know, but every three weeks or so we would dismantle the tent, harness the horse up, and get out on the road looking for somewhere new where we might get some work. We would only go ten or fifteen miles down the road, because that distance was enough for the horse pulling a wagon. It was a big thing for my father too, because he'd have to rebuild the tent as well. Having the horse was all very well, but my father couldn't do much with it. Besides, he'd seen what other travelling men could do with their trucks in England, so, soon after returning home, he bought a van for his work. He'd haul scrap in it, or put it to any use he could, to earn some money.

When we stopped for the night, the first thing my father would do was make the tent, one that would last us as long as we needed to stay put. My brother Paddy and I would be running alongside him, helping to carry the wood. The first job was to cut down the poles that would form the frame, and here hazel wood was the best as it was the easiest to get into place. A long pole would be trimmed of its bark and stuck into a bank. That would hold one end firmly while we watched my father bend the other end over and force it into the ground, making the main stay of the frame – and somewhere to hang things off the floor. This was called the rigging pole. He'd then strip smaller poles until there were enough to start weaving the wattles, as we called them, to form the canopy. Knowing there was now someone living there, the farmer might come by and give us some straw to put inside to make us more comfortable. To finish off the tent, my father would dig a trench around the sides to take away the rainwater. A tent like this could last all winter if it was properly made.

When I was a little older, Paddy and I would have our duties. I would have to get the sticks for the fire in the mornings, and Paddy had to get the water to drink and cook with. The following day I would fetch the water, while Paddy would have to go root in the farmers' hedges for wood for the fire. Doing this meant we learned the layout of the land and all the little places where we could catch our food. My favourite was snaring rabbits. I'd be happy spending time getting my snares ready, waiting to catch some. I'd go down with a set of snares in the evenings and be there for three or four hours. Then, in the morning, I'd go round and check the snares, take the rabbit out if I'd caught one, club it, and carry it home. Sometimes of an evening I'd take the dogs up with me to chase rabbits out of the hedges. I'd send in the little terrier, he'd flush the rabbits out into the open, and the greyhound would race over and pick them up. My father would skin the rabbit (we didn't sell the fur) and gut it and clean it up and my mother would put it in the pan with a few vegetables and boil the whole lot, and that was a lovely dinner.

To get vegetables I would sometimes raid farmers' fields. Of course the farmers would warn us never to steal from them, but I had found a way to take what we needed without being caught. I'd go into the centre of the field where the farmer wouldn't notice anything missing, rather than at the edges where it was obvious, and I'd lift out a few vegetables – just enough for the pot that night. When I brought whatever I'd collected home, no one said to me, 'Where did you get them from?' So as long as it wasn't necessary, then no questions would be asked.

I was very proud of helping to feed my family, and I brought my first rabbit back when I was only 7. The dogs helped me; we had three, all called Jack. We had Auld Jack, who was the boss. When he was 16 we had to get him put down because a weasel blinded him. Then we had young Jack, his son; he was half bulldog, half terrier, and we had him for ten years, until he was killed by a car. We had greyhound Jack and then later on we had a little Jack Russell. All the dogs were there for hunting rabbits and hares. Hare hunting was something I never liked. I don't really know why; whether it was because it involved a lot of running about, or because of the stories we were told round the fire when I was little. I never liked the tales that had me laying awake in bed. One was about some boys who were chasing a hare with their dog, only for the hare to turn into a banshee and kill their dog. Or there was the story where the boys were following a hare and it went out of their sight and turned into an old woman. That one also reminded me of the tale we were told of the little girls who were turned into swans by their stepmother. Some of those stories had a purpose. For instance, we were told never to throw stones at swans – ducks we could chuck stones at, and if we were lucky enough to hit and kill one we could take it home to eat – but never a swan, because of the law.

It was an essential part of a travelling man's life to have a dog and I liked our three – Auld Jack, young Jack and Greyhound Jack – very much. They worked as a team and my father had them together for over twelve years; he always kept dogs rather than bitches, because he wasn't into the hassle of breeding from them. They were pets to us children but their purpose first and foremost was to hunt – they were as essential to our hunting as a fishing rod is to a fisherman. (Talking of fishing, eel rolled in pastry and fried was my favourite dish of all.) The dogs weren't allowed inside the tent, where we slept. They were rough and ready dogs, and had to fend for themselves outside.

When the older boys and the men went out hare coursing I'd try to hang back. It just never seemed to interest me, so I didn't even try to get to like it. The greyhounds were essential for this, because they were the only ones with the speed. They were used for pheasants as well, although we always had to be careful not to take the farmers' birds.

We were careful always not to upset the farmers, because without their help things could be very tough for us. When we left a site we would always clear up properly, because if we didn't, then we'd never be welcome there again. We'd go round the site and bag up any rubbish so there was no sign that we'd been there. It wasn't in our interests to leave it untidy at all, because we'd probably come back that way in four or five months' time and want to feel the farmer was friendly towards us. There would be times when we'd arrive at a site and find it left dirty by someone else – usually someone who'd come from outside our area to use it and so not likely to have to return there. Then we'd end up clearing away their mess.

Whenever a site had been left in a mess, I would feel some prejudice towards us when we arrived. Sometimes when we turned up the farmer – or even the police – would come along and say to us, don't stay there tonight. We knew that if we ignored that advice the likelihood was that a few bricks would be hurled our way later on, that the van windows would be broken. Obviously the family that had stayed there before us had caused trouble, and that hadn't been forgotten. It made no difference if we said we'd not take anything we weren't offered and clear up after ourselves: we were classed the same as the troublemakers. We would have to move on down the road a little bit. Luckily, other farmers would be on the side of the road, and accept us with open arms. They'd give us milk and water, they'd give out straw for the tent, they'd give us all a bit of farm work. It seemed to me that if we behaved like my mother and father – and the older generation – and treated the farmers and their workers with respect, we would probably be given it in return. But because of the behaviour of a few that didn't show them respect, at times we were all treated as one and no longer welcomed where we'd been able to stop before.

Eventually we stopped travelling in a wagon. In 1971 my father bought a caravan to pull on the back of the van. Having the caravan was a big thing for us; we were on the move as my father hunted work, and all went where he had to go. But now we had moved from a tent to a caravan at the side of the road, it was all so different. Like moving from a one-bedroom apartment into a penthouse. We even had a gas cooker in there. My father and mother had the caravan for themselves and the girls. Paddy, me and my younger brother Dave had a bed made for us on a mattress in the back of the van. We'd happily sleep in the back of the van; for us it was like going camping, and it felt like a break from what we'd been used to.

Everything we did in our spare time, we had to provide ourselves, whereas nowadays kids all have video games and things like that. We'd be out all day picking spuds from 6 a.m. until about four in the afternoon. Then straight away we'd have something to eat at home before running outside to play games: football, handball, kick the can – you name it. Even though we'd been working all day, we never felt too tired to play.

A couple of years later another change came that was even more exciting – we moved into a place in Mullingar, where I can remember my mother coming home from the hospital with my sister Maggie. It was a rough area, so bad that much of it has been demolished now, but we were there for a year or so before we moved south to Dublin, where we lived for a short while in Coolock, in the north-east of the city. We never stayed anywhere long enough for me to make friends or even to get to know anyone really.

Nineteen seventy-six was a blistering summer and we stayed right next to the beach for the entire summer. I spent the whole time outdoors, all day in that heat, swimming whenever we could. We had great times there. As well as my family, Chappy was there with all his kids, so we played every kind of game we could out on the beach. We stayed there right through till it was time to move on to start the potato-picking season in County Meath.

Family life was very good. My mother and father were very good to us; they were never too strict and always tried to give us whatever they could afford. They had no education, and so for us those early years were about survival. If my parents could afford a pair of Wellingtons or a pair of shoes or other clothing for us, they'd get them for us. Like every other travelling woman in Ireland in the 1970s, my mother went from door to door knocking for handouts and old clothes, and a lot of those clothes ended up on my back and on the backs of others in the family. That was true for 99 per cent of travelling families throughout Ireland in those years. But even though things were so bad, as a child I wasn't aware of it. As long as we had food I didn't mind how we lived.

From when I was 9 or 10 we were out doing a lot of farm work all over County Dublin, County Louth and County Westmeath. We'd pick potatoes, sprouts, sugar beet – anything the farmers had planted we'd be there to help harvest. I don't remember liking the work but I certainly didn't hate it. Working hard was something that we were just brought up to believe in doing, just as we believed God is God. Work wasn't something that we had to be taught; we knew it almost from our very first breath. We believed that it had to be done, and everyone pitched in to make it easier for the family. For example, my mother didn't just look after all of us, but worked too, selling things at a flea market, the Hill Market in Dublin, on a Saturday.

The time came when my father started thinking how much easier he'd found it to get work in England in the early 1960s. So he went back over to Manchester and when I was 10 we all followed him over. He had also told my mother about how we could get a house over there, and how there were many travelling families – the Joyces, Keenans and Wards – there too. It was so different – I'd never seen a coloured person before, for instance – but living was not a whole lot easier then. The better times had long gone and it was a lot harder to get work than my father had expected. He found work on building sites but having his family with him made the experience harder this time. People were prejudiced against us, although not because we were travellers – we were just Irish to them. There were some who'd call us 'tinkers', which never bothered me much as I didn't really know what it meant, but I was happy when we returned to Ireland. My father sold the van and bought a truck and a car. As he was the only driver, he'd put the car on the back of the truck and hook the caravan on the back of the truck, and set off like that along the roads around Dundalk again.

People in Ireland, I learned, could often be just as prejudiced as the English. We met so few other children from outside the traveller families – mainly the farmers' children who came to see us when we moved onto a site – so we kept very much to ourselves. Not long after moving back from England my father bought a new caravan – well, new to us anyway – and it had a battery in it that could power a little 12-volt black and white television. Sitting in the trailer watching TV by the side of the road was a great thing.

I was happy going back out on the road. Lots of the sites were familiar to me and I knew where to find little hiding places and where to make dens for myself. I never thought life would change; the most my family ever wanted was a nicer car, a nicer caravan. We'd put up somewhere for the winter and be joined by other families who, like us, would travel the roads during the warmer months but rest up for the colder ones. I liked to see new faces, as much as I loved my family I could also get a little sick of the same old thing every day. Even though I had three brothers and three sisters and we all got on like a house on fire, it was still great when someone new to us was nearby. I loved to see someone different pull in beside us, strangers who might be part of the clan but still people we hadn't seen for months. For me the great thing was that our games could be more involved because there were more youngsters joining in.

Come the spring the three or four families would each go their separate ways, and we'd move about, never sure who we'd find ourselves alongside for the night. In those days there was never any trouble between the clans; we were always careful, but the times were easier. It was only when travellers started to give up the travelling life that everything started to get more difficult. That began to happen at the end of the 1970s, when the recession hit and there was little or no work, and the only money my family had coming in was the social security. The lack of work hit everyone, not just travellers.

In 1979 I went to the horse fair at Ballinasloe, over in County Galway, with my father; it was a great experience for me but he didn't enjoy it. My father was the kind of a man who never liked trouble, but there was always trouble at the fairs, so he avoided them if he could. As soon as we saw some fellows picking on each other, trying to provoke a fight, he said, 'Right, Jimmy, we're off,' and that was it. I've never been to a horse fair since.

2

BOXING GLOVES

One thing that never really featured highly in my childhood was school. Like most traveller children, what I needed to learn I learned from my father out in the fields and hedgerows. The only point of going to school, as far as travellers were concerned, was to prepare a child for their Holy Communion and Confirmation by learning about religion.

My first school was the primary school in Mullingar run by the Christian Brothers. Travellers weren't well looked after in school and I discovered it was no different at the one I attended. In the last few years the Christian Brothers' schools have come in for criticism and I'm right behind what has been said about them. Our teacher, Brother Reagan, was a priest, and what he used to do to the small children in his class was not at all nice. He had a thick black strap, what we called the black taffy, and if he felt you needed it, he'd make you stick out your hand and would whack you hard with it. He would do this to kids as young as 6 years old. We never learned anything from him; we just feared and hated him. Traveller children weren't expected to learn; we were simply a nuisance as far as Brother Reagan was concerned and he just wanted us to keep quiet and not bother him. We were never sure of what rules he had, so often we'd get the taffy across our hands for what seemed like nothing at all.

I was taken out of the Christian Brothers' school and sent to the convent school next door. My class was taught by a nun called Sister Mary. She was a saint by comparison with Brother Reagan, but she was as well the loveliest nun I've ever met. All the bad feelings I'd started to have about religious people changed completely when I was in her class. Where Brother Reagan was fierce and angry, Sister Mary was very pleasant, and I felt protected by her. Yet I still didn't learn much with her, always looking forward to being out of the classroom playing.

The school playground was full with my cousins as well as my younger brothers and sisters. One of our cousins, Theresa, was in the class below mine. I didn't see her again until ten years later on, at my brother's wedding – and I had to be reminded who she was. Within a few days of that meeting she'd agreed to marry me.

When I'd been at the school for a while I was moved up into the next class and I stopped learning altogether. But my experience wasn't quite as bad as my brother Paddy's. He and several cousins, boys from the Joyces and Nevins, as well as our cousin Sammy, all roughly the same age, were put into a pre-fab building by themselves at their school. There were no desks, just a few chairs for them to sit on. 'Here you go, lads,' said the teacher, handing them a pack of cards. 'Keep quiet till break time.' That was their education, five days a week. On other days, they'd be led into the playground when they arrived in the morning and told to get on with kicking a ball about, but not to make too much noise or they'd disturb the children from settled families, who were all in class learning.

That I never learned much at school wasn't just down to my being ignored by the teachers, or not caring; it was also because I never stayed in one school long enough. When I'd been at the school in Mullingar for a while, my father came home one night and with absolutely no warning said, 'I'm moving us to Dundalk.' We moved the very next day and after we'd settled into our site I was taken into a school in Dundalk, another school run by the Christian Brothers, but much better than the one in Mullingar. No one chased us to find out why I wasn't at school; the school I had been at had no contact with us, as we had no phone and no forwarding address. No one came round to the site to see if there were any children who should be at school; the system wasn't interested in forcing traveller children to attend school. Why should it be? We weren't going to be doing anything with what we learned; we would be out in the fields long before the other children would be just starting to study for their exams. Travellers wouldn't use what they might have learned because they didn't get jobs that needed an education. That was the attitude people had then. Maybe the authorities also knew that the reason I was going to school was for what I would be given – free uniform and free shoes.

All I could tell my new teachers about what I'd learned was where I went to school and what class I had been in. I couldn't remember what I'd learned and I still couldn't read or write, so whenever I started a new school I was always put into the first class. They never asked me, who was your teacher, how far did you go through the school? Whatever picture books I'd been given were gone, left behind, and that was one of the main reasons my reading and writing never improved. No one at the school ever tried – as far as I know – to contact the previous schools to see what records about me they had. The teachers at each new school seemed to think it was 'easier if we start again, James'. Which meant I never made any progress.

The time that most upset me was when I was taken aside at school and asked about my family. I didn't know what the teacher was getting at until she used the word 'adopted'. I couldn't work out why, but it was because my father called himself Jimmy Quinn and the teachers had my name down as James McDonagh. I didn't know this at the time because nobody explained things like that to me, and I was left to puzzle it out for myself.

We moved again, this time south. I was put in a school, in the middle of Cara Park, a traveller site in Coolock, where there were a few pre-fab buildings in the centre. One of these little units was a school for travellers, and us young lads went there. There were about six or seven of us of the same age going through the last stage of school at the same time, and this is where the one thing that did change things for me came about. The school at least showed some interest in getting me through my religious education, and a little nun educated me for my Confirmation. Sister Clare gave me all the prayers I needed and told me how to respond to the questions I was asked.

The day came for my Confirmation, and that day I wore a blazer. My father and mother were there, watching proudly, as were other traveller families because others were confirmed at the same time. One of them was my friend Turkey's Paddy; we'd got on famously since we'd met. Not long afterwards his family moved on to Newry and he went swimming in a river and drowned. Turkey's Paddy was buried in Dundalk. His mother, Maggie, came over to me at the funeral and said, 'James, you and Paddy will never play together again,' and I cried. I was still only a child and I'd never before experienced losing someone that close to me. I just didn't know what that meant until the moment Turkey's Paddy's mother spoke to me at the funeral. She knew how close the two of us had been, and as a token of that, when she had her next child she called him James.

As soon as I could after I was confirmed, I left school, and we went away and travelled. As a travelling family was mostly moving around in the summer and working in the fields in the autumn, there wasn't a lot of time for me to go to school anyway. I left school at 12. I'd never liked it.

My mother had only sent me to school to be prepared for my Confirmation, and once that was finished she didn't care any more about my education. People care now. As a parent now myself I have very different feelings about education. The times have changed and what was considered OK then would not be allowed now. Back then, traveller kids were considered second class, second rate, and it didn't interest those in charge that we weren't getting an education. Travellers are no longer left behind and ignored in classes; in some schools, like the one my sons went to in Dundalk, there are classes just for travellers. Some see this as special treatment but I don't, because I think traveller children have a long way to go to catch up with settled children, who are used to the idea of school, expect it, and welcome it. It will take a long time for education to become a habit for all traveller families. You can't make that happen just by wanting it; you have to change the way everybody else thinks about it too, and that is a long-term project.

BOXING GLOVES

In later life I taught myself to read and write, but as a young boy the only thing I liked about school was learning about religion. All traveller families are religious, some more than others perhaps, but they all believe in God. Some may be sarcastic about it, they may do wrong, but they also believe in Holy Mother Mary and in Jesus Christ. That has never left me; as an adult I have even been on pilgrimages overseas, to Fatima in Portugal, for instance. A lot of travellers go to Lourdes. I try to attend Mass every Sunday. I believe in Heaven – that when someone has been good they will go there – and I believe in Hell. I believe in a lot of angels. The Holy Trinity is tattooed on my back. Religion is probably the most important constant in traveller life, and all families bring their children up to believe in God and to go to Mass. A newborn child must be christened, because travellers believe that a child doesn't prosper or improve until they get that original sin taken away from them by being baptised into the Church. We pray for those who have died, we pray for their souls, we pray for each other. My wife is a very religious person. Theresa will say the Rosary every day and she will never miss Mass. She'll walk five or even ten miles to attend.

Although I'd left school I was still unable to go and join my father in his work – I was too young – so instead I had to work at a training centre for young travelling kids. AnCo was the name of the organisation, and they would teach me a skill that would enable me to become an apprentice in a job. I chose carpentry but it was never really my thing. I did it for a while, mostly because I was paid £30.30 a week to stay on there at AnCo.

The first week I had that money in my hands I went out to spend it right away. When we were doing the farming work, all we ever got was pocket money because all that we were earning was needed to keep the home going. It meant so much to me to have my own money to spend at last. I knew what I wanted to buy first: a bike. That way I could get out, go anywhere I wanted. The second week, I bought a tape deck so I could listen to music. The third week, I bought some clothes: Shakin' Stevens was big then with his hit 'This Ole House' and I bought some clothes like his. White trainers, tight jeans, a Levi jacket, black shirt, white tie: that was Shakin' Stevens's look on his album cover and I got it. But it wasn't a Shakin' Stevens record I bought first; it was Rod Stewart's 'Baby Jane'. I liked Rod, still do, and country and western too, and we'd dance to the records at the teenage disco that was held on the site once a week. I was happy with what I was doing: I was earning some money, I spent Friday nights at the disco, and the rest of the weekend hunting. And I went boxing.

I'd started boxing for two reasons. The first was that I hated being pushed around by other kids, and from a young age found myself bullied. Certain settled kids in Mullingar were bullies; they were a clan of their own, and a little gang of them would go about the place trying to find someone to pick on. They'd never value anything we said or did. That has all changed since those days, and when my sons were at school they learned that settled kids often look up to traveller kids. But it wasn't like that when I was young. If a game of football or of handball was going on, I'd go to join in and these kids – who weren't playing themselves – would stop me, push me off the field, and hit me. If they were playing and it was our turn to play, they'd push me away, kick me up the arse, shove me, slap me on the head. They would hit me hard enough to make me cry, and crying is embarrassing when you're that age. No one would stop them because they knew that they'd get the same thing if they tried.

It wasn't just settled kids who were the problem. I remember one time at Cara Park, I was playing with two friends on the roof of a pre-fab. Another kid came along, older than us but shorter, and told us to stay up there or he'd punch us. We were that petrified of him that we stayed up there on the roof even when he went away, and only crept down when it got to about two in the morning. There we were, the three of us, all taller than him, and we still wouldn't come down. That's the power bullies have over people.

I didn't have many friends then. I'd make friends easily, but if we didn't move off after a few weeks, then their families did. When you're that age you really look for someone to be your friend, especially if you feel you're picked on otherwise. So perhaps it wasn't a surprise that I fell in with some people who lived near Cara Park, in Belcamp House, a mansion that later burned down. They were a charismatic Christian group and I started going there just for the fun of it and then really got into attending the prayer meetings and other events they organised. I made some good friends there and for a while I became very serious about being involved in their kind of Roman Catholicism. For two years I was going to prayer meetings on Tuesdays and Thursdays, as well as Mass on Sundays. Saturdays we'd meet for bible study. It's a surprise that I had time for anything else.

My greatest friends at Belcamp House were an American family called Cullins. Brendan Cullins was around my age and became my particular friend. The family moved back to the States and – it just goes to show the difference an education can make – Brendan went on to be a brain surgeon, while I ended up someone who goes to country lanes to bash people in the face for a living.

As kids we'd always boxed a bit. We couldn't always play football or whatever game we wanted, but boxing was something else we could do near to the site. When we came back from picking spuds or wherever we'd been, if there wasn't time to run off and get a game going, we could stay by the trailer and box. I'd always known I wasn't very good at football, much as I liked to run about. I was always last to be picked to go on someone's team, and when there's fifteen to twenty kids standing on the pitch waiting to get the game going, this can be embarrassing. I was always the last one chosen because everyone knew that no matter how hard I tried I couldn't kick a ball. It made me feel some kind of wimp that I couldn't kick a football straight. To this day I think I must have been the worst footballer of any traveller in the world. Trying to play handball was no better. No one would play doubles with me, even though I liked the game. They didn't want to waste their time because again I couldn't play it.

Just about every sport I was rubbish at; so when I realised that I could throw out my two hands well, I was pleased. I don't know whether people were happy for me that I'd found something I could do, or if they were just being polite, when they said, 'You know, James, you're not bad at that boxing there,' but that motivated me. I'd finally found something that I enjoyed and that people liked seeing me doing. It would be big-headed of me to say I was good at boxing right from the start, but I'd found something that I was better at than most other people. I only took it up in the first place because I could do it and because I thought that if I was any good I could use it to stop being bullied – I had no idea where it would take me in the end. I just wanted to be able to look after myself in years to come.

My father never had a fist-fight in his life. His brother Chappy was known as a man to have had a few fights, but not my father. If my father got into trouble, Chappy would step in and take his place or go and sort it out. He had done a bit of boxing – or a bit of fighting, shall I say – but no training. So I'm not sure why my brother Paddy and I took to it so well. I just know we did.

When I was 10 and Paddy a year or so older, we were given boxing gloves for Christmas. Paddy loved boxing from the moment he started; he still loves it to this day, and although he's a bit old to do the training now, he still has the head for it and knows what he's doing. As Paddy's sparring partner, it took me a while to do more than just stand there and block his punches. But eventually I did, and that's when people noticed I could box quite well. So I was sent along to a club to train and learn to box properly.

Paddy started to box regularly at a local gym in Dundalk. When he went for his training sessions I would sometimes go down there with him. At first I felt out of place – the other boys seemed more powerful than me and I was long and skinny then – but after a while I got to like it. I started feeling fitter from all the training I did and once I had learned to protect myself properly I really started to enjoy the boxing itself.

I joined the Dealgan Boxing Club and I trained there for about a year and a half before we moved too far away for me to travel there easily. Then, when we moved to Cara Park, I carried on my training at the Darndale Boxing Club in Coolock, where they produced great boxers like Joe Lawler, who fought in the 1986 Olympics. There I learned how to move when boxing, how to breathe – not as simple as it sounds – and it was there I would have my first fights. The first thing the trainer, Joe Russell, taught me at Darndale was to breathe in through my nose, out through my mouth. 'James,' Joe said, 'every chance you get, hold back, get the breath in your body. Stand off a little, not so far he notices but far enough to give you a little time to breathe. Take every chance you can. In through the nose, out through the mouth. Don't *show* you're breathing, like this' – he would breathe heavily and fast through his mouth – 'don't let them know. Just step back and be on your foot, be on your back foot, be on your toe.' Joe would demonstrate by standing tall and breathing deeply through his nose. 'Side step. When you feel tired, you know, just step back a little bit. Drop the hand. Let the blood flow back in. If you hold it up for five minutes it gets tired. So you have to just pull it back in and relax.' Now Joe was talking about fighting in a ring, where there are breaks to let you recover your breath and lower your guard. Years later, when I was fighting out in the air with no ropes and no breaks, his advice was still the best I'd been given. Rest, and breathe, whenever you can.

The boxing club itself was a place I liked to go to, because the people there had an attitude towards us travellers that was completely different from what we'd encountered at school. Schools hadn't been very good to us, whereas the boxing club welcomed us in. Having someone teach me who encouraged me to improve every time I came in – a new experience after my years at school – meant not only that I started to enjoy my boxing, but that learning came easily to me. In addition, the training did a lot for my strength and my physique. I found aggression that I didn't have outside in the world would come to me when I was in the ring. At first I wondered where this came from, because outside the ring I thought I was a normal person, but when I stepped into the ring it was a different story. Perhaps it was because with the gloves on and someone in front of me wanting to hit me, I became a different person.

Young traveller lads on the sites we stayed on were often keen to take up the sport because it meant they could say to themselves and their friends, 'I can handle myself, I can box.' Sometimes boxing clubs would have as many as ten or twelve travellers as members, but as usual they would come and go, depending on where their families were living and working and whether or not they could keep up the training. Me and Paddy were the most persistent two in the club; we stuck it out for a good few years, Paddy longer than I did. My younger brother Dave joined us in the club and he too was a good boxer, but he never kept it up the way Paddy did, or went out onto the street with it the way I did.

At the club I made good progress and was paired up with Joe Lawler as my sparring partner. He was about my age but a lot lighter than me and a lot smaller too. To be honest, Joe was my biggest nightmare there. He had a right-hand punch that I couldn't seem to avoid, and when he hit me with it I was always taken by surprise because it was phenomenally hard. He would jump up slightly and sling his hand forward, and I'd see it coming at me, riding over the top of his reach until it connected with my head – *bam*. I don't think he'd be allowed to use it now, but he'd just sink it on my head and I'd feel my brain pounding. Joe was brilliant: I watched him win nearly fifty fights with a knock-out, and in all of them that right hand of his made the difference. I used to dream about that punch, it preyed on my mind so much.

The first time I stepped into the ring for a competitive fight I wasn't successful, but as it was my first fight I hadn't had any experience, so I wasn't disappointed that I lost that one, and besides I knew I'd fought very well. But the next fights went my way: I won every one of the following thirteen, both club and competition fights. Ten boxers would be picked from each club and put into the ring to fight each other. The biggest fights for me were when I fought for Dublin against Galway, Cork and Limerick in the under-18 County League as a little scrawny ten-stone welterweight.

I didn't win my last County League fight, though, against a guy from Omagh, in County Tyrone. A Northern Ireland champion, he was four years older than me, bigger than me, stronger than me; and at that age those four years can make a lot of difference. But everyone said I had balls to go into the ring with the guy and so I felt some confidence before the fight. And I went into the ring and fought well; although I lost I didn't embarrass myself. My trainer said, 'James, well, you know you lost, though to me it was a fifty/fifty fight but the judges went against you.' I knew he was trying to pick me back up, but the feeling of losing that fight was pretty bad. But at least I knew I'd been beaten by someone bigger, stronger and more experienced. If I'd lost to someone I didn't feel had those advantages over me, I'd have been almost suicidal. I understood then how much I didn't like losing, and it was something I hadn't realised until it happened.

I didn't yet think I could make anything of myself as a boxer. I enjoyed it and wanted to carry on but at that time it wasn't something I thought I could carry on for ever. This was down to my family life; I knew that at any moment we might move away from Dublin and I'd no longer be coming into the gym. I had a couple of competitive fights coming up, one in Dublin and then – if that went well – a tournament in Leeds where I'd be representing Ireland – when my father told me we were leaving the city.

We had been living in a little traveller housing scheme in Coolock, but my father told me he needed to move again in his hunt for work, because there was none anywhere in the Dublin area. I didn't know it at the time, and it wouldn't have meant anything to me then, but Ireland was going through a deep recession. Back then most travellers didn't know what a recession was. Now they can see that a recession affects all walks of life, but at that time, like most people, they didn't know anything about politics or economics; all they knew was about surviving, day-to-day living. My father decided that we'd try our luck in England again, so my time in the boxing club was over.

Some years later I learned that there was more to it than this, that my father had had a dispute with my trainers at the club. I don't know who this dispute was with, and I don't know what it was about, but he had fallen out with someone at the club. He told me many years later that it was due to some perceived favouritism at the club – that he wanted me to face someone else but the club had reserved that fight for another boxer, and he felt I was being overlooked. I don't know the ins and outs of all this and I wouldn't like to speculate, but I don't resent what happened. All I do know is that I was due to take part in the biggest fight of my life so far – I would have won a national title if I'd won that fight – and we were going to move abroad before it could happen.

I wish now that I'd been given a chance to pursue that boxing career, to see whether it would have taken me along a different path than the one I ended up on, and whether it would have got me a career inside the ring. I believe I could have done something with the boxing. I believe that I could have faced the challenge. I wasn't a sports person, so to find a sport I liked, one where I could control the opposition and do what I wanted with them, made boxing very exciting to me. I was good as a boxer and I wanted to carry on with it. I don't know how far I could have gone but I would have loved to have had the chance to find out. Perhaps then I wouldn't have found myself boxing out on the street.

3

ENGLAND

My father hitched up the caravan and we all set off to England on 13 April 1984. The ferry runs from Dublin to Holyhead in Anglesey, off the north-west coast of Wales, but we weren't expecting to stay in Wales for any length of time but to drive straight on into England. When we got off the ferry, though, my father was taken to one side; it turned out that he was banned from returning to England after he was imprisoned there in the 1960s. He was supposed to stay out of the country for twenty-five years, he was told. He said he had no idea that the ban was still in force but no one took any notice of what he said and he was taken off by the police and put into a cell to await an appearance in court.

We were stuck in Holyhead. We couldn't leave without my father, as we didn't know if he was going to be locked up again, told to leave the country, or what. My mother was in distress. We got in touch with some of my father's relatives and they came to see how he was doing and whether or not there was anything they could do to help us. It was my uncle Johnny Boy, my cousin Joe Joyce, and his cousin Tim Joyce who came to see us. Paddy was 17, I was 16, and the three of them took us to the pub. We had a few drinks and then went to see my father. The policeman who took us to the cell said, 'Lads, there's no problem, really. He'll go to court and they'll deactivate the banning order and he can come out. If he'd committed crimes in Ireland it would be different, but as it stands there'll be no problem.' And he was right: after a couple of days my father was released and we were back on the road again.

We headed to a little village called Wing in Buckinghamshire, between Aylesbury and Leighton Buzzard. This is where my uncle and cousins had come from to see us in Holyhead. We stayed there on their site with them for a couple of months and then moved on to Eye, outside Peterborough, where we stayed in a lay-by.

My father and my cousin would go out looking for work together – we call it hawking. They'd spend the day hawking and then, if we were lucky, they'd come back having got themselves some work for the next day. It might be shifting something in the van, or laying tarmac on someone's drive. If anyone needed labourers, Paddy and I would do that. They were the foremen – we were the workforce, the ones actually doing the work. Except when it came to laying tarmac; you had to be skilled to do that, not because the work required it, but because the skill came in making money out of it. The thinner the layer of tarmac you laid the less your outlay, and that's where you made some profit. The older men were far more experienced than me and my brother at getting the thinnest layer possible, so they did that work, while we cleared the ground and kept the tools hot in the fire. That's not to say we'd do a bad job – my father and Joe were proud of the work they did – but we weren't doing it for love but for money. And once we had one house in a street getting their drive done, then Paddy and I would be up and down the road, asking people if they wanted theirs done too, 'because we're in the area doing your neighbour's drive and we've a little tar left over'. That worked a treat every time.

Meanwhile I found a boxing club to go to, the local one in Leighton Buzzard, in Bedfordshire. When I had warmed up a bit my first time there, the trainers asked if I'd go in the ring and spar with their top boxer, a 17-year-old ABA season champion. I don't know why they asked me. Maybe they'd run out of sparring partners for him and wanted fresh meat. I suppose I can't have looked much of a threat to him, as he was massive, like a fully grown man, with a crewcut and tattoos, and there was me, a scrawny thing of about ten stone, slightly younger than him to boot. But I'd forgotten to mention to them how much fighting I'd done in Dublin, so I had that up my sleeve, and when we got into the ring I punched this lad around the ropes, and in two or three rounds I took him apart. I kept him away from me, so he couldn't touch me, and when I stepped in and hit him I got my punches away cleanly. He was livid but the trainers were delighted. They wanted a proper test for the guy, and they thought they'd found another boxer for their stable. 'Have you boxed much before?' someone now bothered to ask me. 'Well, a little,' I told him. 'A year or two in Dublin. I won a few fights for the club.' He studied me a bit. 'We'd like to enter you for some fights here, you know.'

Of course I was interested and wanted to fight, but my father moved us on again to another site and I never went back to that club again.

Throughout that summer we found enough work, and then it was spud season, so we went back to the farms to lift potatoes. During the winter we would go door to door, sharpening lawnmowers and shears, kitchen knives – anything to keep us going till the spring, when we moved to Wisbech for the strawberry picking. Meanwhile other families came to join us, another uncle and cousins, and some of the Nevins too.

Moving around England wasn't that easy. When we left a site there may have been seven or eight caravans in all if we moved together, and the police would come out and escort us out of their area. When we hit the boundary of, say, Derbyshire, the local police would be waiting there, and they would barricade us in a convoy and try to make us drive another forty miles or so to the other side of the county, because they didn't want to have the problem of travellers in their area. Wherever we stopped they stopped, and from time to time a new police guard would move us on out of that area too. This would go on until we pulled into a public car park or the forecourt of a garage, and then some of the travellers, who knew their rights, would tell the police: we're in a garage, we're staying here, we're parking in the lay-by, we're entitled to pull into a lay-by, and the police would have to move off. We'd stay there for a few days and then look for a more permanent site. The best campsites to move into were the council-run ones, because a court order was needed to get you off. We could fight the court order for a certain length of time, and we learned to play the system; we'd be in a camp for four, maybe five weeks, the court order would give us a certain day to move off by, so we'd leave the day before, the barriers would be dismantled, and two days later we'd move back again. The council would have to start the legal proceedings again.

One time we moved onto a site and found ourselves next to some gypsies. I'd never met gypsies before and I wanted to see if their ways were as different from ours as I'd been told by my mother and father. I was with gypsy lads my age and we seemed totally alike all day – until it came to dinner. 'Come over and eat with us,' they said. 'We're having hedgehog.' And not hedgehog roasted over a fire, but hedgehog buried an inch or two down in the ground and then cooked under the fire, in the earth. We went home and talked non-stop about their ways, the little things we wouldn't notice, which they laughed about, and their eating habits. 'Did you see what they were eating?' To this day I don't know any Irish traveller who would eat a hedgehog.

One of the gypsy families were Scottish. Alfie Stewart and his family were the nicest people in the world and one of the daughters caught my eye as well. But when my brother also took notice of another gypsy girl on the site and came home that evening, my father said, 'No, Paddy, you're not seeing her. We're just too different.' And that was that: Paddy left the girl alone. My father was right, and I decided not to go after her either.

While we were at the site there was a wedding between two gypsy families, but it wasn't one that either family had looked for. A boy on the site had taken to a girl and they were always sitting together, walking together, always chatting away. Their families must have known something was up but we knew nothing of how the families felt about it until one morning when we were riding out to the field to start picking. The farmer would come by and we'd all climb into the back of his van to be driven out to whichever field we were going to start working in, and the farmer had only gone about halfway down the lane when a car pulled up and out hopped the boy. He came to the back of the van and opened the doors. He saw the girl and gestured for her to come out. 'You, come on, you're coming with me, now.' She didn't say anything but stared, so he added, 'Look, make your mind up, are we going to go and do it, or what?' The girl looked around at us all, then said, 'Yeah,' grabbed her lunch box and scrambled out of the van and ran off with the lad to his car.

The next we heard was they'd driven up to Gretna Green, just over the border with Scotland, and got married. They reappeared a week later and told their families. Neither family was particularly pleased but there was nothing they could do about it now.

After the season was over we moved on. To Leighton Buzzard, then somewhere in the Thames Valley, back to Wisbech, on to Wellingborough – anywhere my father had heard there might be work. We didn't stay long in any of those places because once we arrived we'd hear from other travellers that they'd been there for a while and the pickings were slim, or they'd just left somewhere else and it was better than here. So off we'd go again. This time we went to Bedford, and it was while we were there that Paddy asked Kathleen, back in Mullingar, to marry him. He would travel back to Dublin to go up and see her and they would talk on the phone all the time too.

On 28 April 1985 we were all back in Ireland for Paddy and Kathleen's wedding. Three hundred people came. Now a traveller wedding is always an event, because it's one of the few times when travellers from different clans will come together to enjoy the day. We'll drink and dance and gamble and it'll be a great occasion. Of course there are some funny things too; if you went into the hall, you'd see the women on one side of the room and the men on the other. No man will go and sit with a woman, even if she's his own wife; he'd be called sissy – and worse – by the other men. This was true of any kind of party or even an evening in the pub, with the men and women sitting in different places all evening, although it's not so often the case nowadays. Twenty-five couples would walk in, and once through the door the men and women would go in different directions, so there'd be twenty-five men up at the bar and twenty-five women sitting on the far side of the room. The only meeting point would be the dance floor in the middle. As a boy I didn't really notice because that's how it had always been. But now if I went to the pub with the wife, I would sit with her, because times are changing.

So, at Paddy's wedding, as a young boy I stood at the bar with all the other men. It was then that I saw a girl in a sky-blue skirt-suit sitting on the other side of the hall. I'd seen her in the church earlier and wondered who she was, so I turned to my cousin Michael and asked him. 'You don't know her?' he said. I looked at her again and said, 'No', and Michael clapped me on the shoulder and said, 'That's Cowboy's daughter, Theresa.'

My cousin, Theresa. The little girl who'd been at the convent school in Mullingar. I hadn't seen her since we were about 5 years old. 'Oh, that's my cousin?' I said casually. She could see me looking at her and she looked back at me shyly. So I picked up my courage and walked over and asked her to dance. 'Yes, James,' she replied, because of course she knew who I was.

And that was it. We danced, and I wouldn't let anyone else dance with her. She didn't want to dance with anyone else. I didn't know the girl on 27 April, and by the 29th I'd asked her to marry me.

It wasn't that straightforward, of course. I spoke to my grandfather first, and asked him if he would ask Theresa's father, Hughie, if I could marry Theresa. My grandfather was something of a matchmaker anyway, so he was delighted to have to go and talk to Hughie. He went out and came back a short while later. 'Well?' I said, eager to hear what Hughie had said. My grandfather gave nothing away. 'Come down to the house,' he told me. 'Why? What did she say?' I was worried. Had Theresa changed her mind? Had Hughie told her she couldn't marry me? 'Come up and ask her yourself,' my grandfather replied, and that gave me no comfort at all. I still couldn't work out if that was a yes or a no.

We walked over to Hughie's house. He was waiting but I wanted to stand outside. I heard my grandfather go in and say, 'Hughie, James out there wants to know if he can marry your daughter Theresa.' Hughie said, 'I don't know, I don't. It's up to her.' Theresa was called for and she became very bashful as my grandfather explained why he was there and why I was standing about outside. After a while my grandfather got a bit fed up and said bluntly to Theresa, 'Well, do you want to marry him?' She said, 'Yeah, I do,' and so from that moment we were engaged. I was three months away from my eighteenth birthday.

When the wedding was over I had to go back to England with my family, so I worked hard for a month and saved up as much money as I could before I went back to see Theresa again. We went to a jeweller together to pick out her engagement ring. Over the next year I'd come back as often as I could to see her, and a year to the day from Paddy's wedding we got married, in Mullingar. I had the full gear on, the wedding suit, a shirt with frills – this was the 1980s – while Theresa wore a beautiful white dress. I look back on the photos now and she was stunning but ... I was embarrassing. Our wedding party was a party like Paddy's, with all our cousins – including the Joyces and the Nevins – having a great time.

Now this girl had seen me only five times in the year, and two days after her wedding she had to leave her family behind and move to London, where I was now living on a site, to be with me. She had never lived in a caravan; she had been born in a house and lived there all her life. She'd never travelled the roads like I had, and here she was ready to move from her family home into a twelve-foot by six-foot caravan for what turned out to be the next nine years. I was six-foot two, with a twenty-six-inch waist. I was the scrawniest, thinnest, ugliest little thing in the world. And the luckiest, and the happiest.

We started out in Hackney, east London, and then moved up to Cambridge. We travelled with my aunt Winnie and her husband Jimmy Kerrigan. Jimmy and I started to work together; we'd drive around and spot cars that looked as if they were going to be scrapped – cars untouched in driveways, cars clearly undriven outside houses, grass growing over the wheels – and go and offer to scrap them for the owner. We'd explain that the scrap value was so low we couldn't offer them more than twenty or thirty quid to take them away to the scrapyard, but once we had the cars (and we always took the car's papers too, telling the owners we needed those to be able to scrap the vehicle legally) we'd take them down to London and sell them as second-hand cars. We used to get anything between two and three hundred quid for each car, and we were handling two or three a day.

Sometimes people didn't want to sell the car. We'd then explain that the only thing of value in it was the gearbox, and that we could take this out and reuse parts of it, but that we had to take the whole car away as then it really would be only fit for scrap. Somehow this seemed to work and while we might have to pay a bit more – say forty or fifty quid – we were still getting a good return once we got the car back to London.

This nice little earner came to an end in a very odd way. The money we made depended on us being able to find cars well outside London and then bring them back and make the profit there. We'd set up home in an area and scour the place for cars before we moved on to somewhere else. One night Jimmy, Winnie, my uncle Davey and his family, along with me and Theresa, had set up in a field – a really lovely place, not far outside Cambridge – and we thought it was going to be fine there. Some travellers were already there, people we knew of but hadn't met before, the Rooneys, and in particular Dan Rooney, who was a well-known boxer. The day we moved in they were just pulling out, which to our minds made it even nicer, as we had such a lovely spot all to ourselves.

The setting was perfect and the day was made complete when Theresa announced that she was pregnant and that I was going to be a father. Of course, we men went off to the pub and left the women behind while we celebrated, and by the time we returned to the caravans it was midnight. But instead of finding Theresa already asleep when I went in, the place was empty. I stepped back outside, when from out of one of the other trailers my aunt Winnie appeared and hissed to us, 'There's people in the camp ... men ... they're banging on the walls and kicking the doors.' We looked around and couldn't see anyone, but then it was very dark. 'We can't see nothing,' I said. 'I'm telling you they're there,' Winnie said. Now she sounded worried and we too started thinking, maybe there is someone out there, and they want people gone from this field. Maybe we should move on. 'Shall we move on down the road, lads?' Jimmy said. 'Only a short way, mind,' he added. We knew that there was another camp only a mile or so away. We agreed and were hitching up the caravans when suddenly Winnie shrieked, 'Jimmy, there, beside you!' We looked round and there was this horrific figure standing over him – seven foot tall, white-faced, with a black hat and cloak. We dropped everything and ran for the caravan door. Davey was last and as he came in we saw his T-shirt had been torn across his back, revealing deep scratches in his flesh.

Suddenly thudding and banging started up on the side of the trailer. We all sat there quaking, I don't mind telling you, and waited to see what happened next. None of us wanted to go and deal with it but every time we peered outside we saw nothing. Still the thumping carried on and – as soon as it was light – we hitched up the vans and drove south to London. Back in London, that was the end of the car-scrapping business as I found some other work to do and stayed put.

The only time we went back out into the country was in February 1987, when we moved onto Cheltenham Racecourse – we smashed a fence to get on the course – for two weeks for my sister's wedding. She was married the same day – in the same church – as two of our cousins from the Joyce side of the family. Joyces from Ireland and Joyces from London, known to everyone as the Bronx Joyces. After the wedding we moved to the same area of town as the Bronx Joyces, Peckham in south-east London, and lived on a site on Consort Road.

Theresa had our first son, JJ, in room 13 on the thirteenth floor of Guy's Hospital (the same room where our second son would be born five years later) and she came out of hospital and brought him home on St Patrick's Day 1987. My father came to see his first-born grandchild while I went and bought a carry-out – a large amount of drink – and we had a celebration round the fire outside, a singsong, and many drinks. It was a great thing for us and for my parents: their first grandchild.

Now we were staying in one place I took up boxing again. I joined the Lynn Boxing Club in Peckham when we moved there, and I was in the same gym as a boxer called Henry Akinwande, who went on to become WBO World Heavyweight Champion in 1996–7. Back then Henry was just starting out but I had only one sparring session with him. I hadn't been in the ring for years, but I was young and fit, and at that age – and I never smoked – my brain was telling me to do things, and my body was still just fit enough to follow, so I did it. I never lost the basics I needed to box properly; it was like riding a bike, and once I'd learned the skills I never lost them. I didn't manage to surprise Henry but we had a good session and I liked knowing that I could still fight well when I had to.

With a young family I didn't have the time to go to the club. I'd start work on building sites early in the morning and after a day's labouring – from eight till six every day, with a half-day on Saturdays – I was too tired to go to the gym to train. The training and the boxing had to take second place to earning a living to support my family. We were still moving about, living on sites which might be a side road, a dead end, a lay-by, or a derelict yard – all around Peckham and the Old Kent Road. A councillor named Ian Ritchie came and asked us to move, and we told him we weren't going anywhere, so he said, right, if you're not going to move I'm going to get you porta-loos. He was a nice guy and true to his word, because once a week the council would empty the portaloos and refill them with new disinfectant, and provide big rolls of paper. We thought that was a great thing: we had toilets.

To begin with I was a labourer, earning £187.50 a week. The people I worked for were what I called the thickest – by which I mean stubborn – in the world. I'd get a half-hour break when I was digging and they'd time me. On the dot I had to be back down in the hole and carrying on. No conversation at all. So when someone told me there was a new company starting up that was looking to employ people, and they were paying over £200 a week, I said, that's for me, anything's better than this. The company was working in Vauxhall, and I went into the building site and spoke to someone. He was from Cork and I could tell at once that he liked a drink. His boss, Seamus Keene, was from Kilkenny, and I saw right away that he was an absolute gentleman. They told me they had two vacancies, ideal for me and my father, so we took the jobs and were now earning £225 or £230 a week and working fewer hours.

One morning we arrived for work and there was no sign of the man from Cork. He couldn't be contacted either, so Seamus came out to talk to the group of us as we stood there. 'Any of you lads working as a ganging man before?' Well, I didn't need any more encouragement than that and stepped out and said, 'I have.' Seamus asked, 'Who did you work for?' I thought of the biggest name in construction at the time and told him McGinleys, to which he nodded. 'That'll do,' he said. 'I'll put you on seven quid an hour.' 'Fine by me,' I replied. 'Is that permanent or short-term?' I didn't want to do short-term work just until the position was filled by someone more quali-fied. 'No, the job's yours. The old boy's gone,' said Seamus. And that was good enough for me.

Of course I hadn't done that job before but I had listened to what we were told to do and I just said the same things now to the other guys. I'd go up to the office, get my orders for the day, come down and tell the lads to get on with it, and then I'd muck in and give them a hand. I wasn't going to sit back and watch them do it, just because I was getting a pound an hour more. The company that we were subcontracted to seemed happy with what I was doing, Seamus Keene told me, and after a couple of months he came onto the site and took me to one side. 'James, will you do me a favour?' he said.

'Would you be interested in taking a new job, moving up the ladder?' 'Oh, yes,' I replied. 'What's that?' I still didn't know how to read, write, spell, anything, so I was really chancing it now. Seamus asked me to be contract supervisor – going around with timesheets to all the building sites, where we had the contracts, going round the site getting the timesheets signed, stamped, and then taking them back to his office, which was a little shed behind the back of his house. Seamus was so busy he needed someone he trusted to do this side of the business for him, so within only a few short weeks of joining the firm I now found myself in a suit, with a briefcase and a six-week-old Audi – I even had one of the first types of mobile phone, the old briefcase phone, but there was no one to ring me or anyone I could ring, so that was a waste.

The job itself, though, was fantastic. I'd be in the office at six on a Monday morning to pick up the timesheets, which I'd distribute round the sites; then I'd collect them on Wednesday (on Tuesday I could do what I wanted) and take the wages round on Thursday and Friday. For this Seamus paid me £800 a week, plus another £100 each week for expenses. I didn't know what he meant by expenses, so he explained that it was for me to spend when I was 'entertaining clients'. Well, I had no clients but my dad and my cousins, so that's what I spent it on.

I wasn't college-educated, but I was streetwise, and I think that's what Seamus saw in me and what he wanted. I knew how to bullshit; I knew how to tell a person what they wanted to hear in order to get somewhere, if I was pricing a job, or estimating the cost of materials, or something else like that for the company. I'd tell people what they wanted to hear and if the people on the building site liked what they heard, they'd give me the work. But I faced a big challenge. To do the job I knew I had to find a way round the problem of being unable to read and write.

But years of not reading had taught me how to get round this one. For a start, I always got someone else to fill in the timesheets. I was supposed to hand them to the secretary on the site and wait while she filled them in. Instead I'd go into the site office, chat with the staff, then leave them the forms, saying I'd be back in an hour for them. I'd make up an excuse – 'I've no time, I've got to get on site and see one of my guys' – and then I'd walk round the site, chat with the lads, come back and collect the forms. I'd pretend to look through them and say things like, 'Are you sure about those hours?', pretending I knew exactly what I was talking about. I'd get the boss to sign them, then I'd do the same all over again at seven or eight sites, until I had all the forms completed. There were a few times when I was nearly caught out, but I always tried to pick up little things as I went along. If I had to fill the timesheets in myself, I'd pull into a car park and I'd look at one of them and copy it closely, deliberately getting a spelling wrong, changing some of the hours about so they didn't seem identical, and other little tricks like that.

Things went smoothly for six or seven months until some-one bought into the company and decided that they didn't need someone doing my job, and they were all for getting rid of me. Just as that was about to happen, though, the wages were stolen from the van I was driving. Twenty-five grand gone just like that. They paid me some wages and some 'compensation' and sent me on my way; I found out from Seamus later that some of the other members of the company had organised the theft, and this only came to light when someone else attacked them with a baseball bat.

Seamus still liked me and now he hired me as his driver. Meanwhile my father – who had also left the company – bought a lorry, and when I wasn't driving Seamus around I was doing removals and haulage with him. I realised I was going to have to learn to read and write, so I started actually teaching myself by reading the sports pages and recognising numbers or names, or names of famous actors I knew on the telly. For instance, I'd see the words 'John Wayne' in a caption below his photograph and then check another picture of him to see if the same words were there too. But I wasn't able to spell his name unless I copied it out, and my spelling is still terrible, though it's far better than it was. The difficulty I had with all this made both Theresa and me determined that our son – and the second one on the way – would not struggle in the same way. Both boys went to school until they were 16 and got the basics of reading, writing and spelling, and both of them can use computers. A few years ago many a traveller couldn't even say his alphabet, but we wanted to make sure that wasn't going to be how it was for our boys.

So, back in 1992, my father and I were doing a bit of haulage and I was driving for Seamus. We were making good money from it – a few hundred pounds a week – and I was content living in Peckham, doing what I was doing, with no plans to change things. If what happened next hadn't occurred, then maybe I'd have my own business now, and probably would never have gone back to Ireland. I might even have got back into education of some sort, perhaps night school, to help me. The bare-knuckle boxing might not have happened.

4

THE BEGINNING ...

I saw my first bare-knuckle fight when I watched a tape of a fight that took place in Crossmaglen, in County Armagh, in August 1990. The fight was between Dan Rooney and Denis 'Aney' McGinley. We learned about it when we were outside the trailer and some lads drove onto the site. Whenever travellers came onto a new site they'd always go up to the people already there, have a chat, find out who was on the site and what the work was like in the area. I expected them to ask us those sorts of questions. Instead they chatted for a while and then one of them asked, 'Have you heard about this bare-knuckle fight?' I didn't know what they were talking about, so they filled me in. They said it was coming up soon and they were driving back to Northern Ireland to go and see it. 'Someone'll video it. Maybe you can get a copy of the tape,' one of the guys added.

When I was next by a pay phone I rang some of the relatives and asked them to send me a copy of the tape once they could get hold of it. It was about a month later when the package arrived.

Aney McGinley was an up and coming young man who wanted to make a name for himself as a boxer. He could fight, I could see that right away on the tape: his stance, the way he threw his punches. Dan Rooney was the seasoned champion of the era, the latest in a long generation of fighting travelling men. The fight was a staged one but the video camera ended up following people round for three days because Dan Rooney couldn't get a flight and left Aney McGinley waiting for three days for him to turn up. When Rooney did get there the fight lasted about fifteen minutes. It was give and take on both sides, and in the end each man claimed that he'd won. There was talk of them staging a rematch but nothing ever came of that.

I thought the referees didn't do their job properly; they let the crowd close in on them too much, so the people watching and those filming couldn't clearly see the action. When the fight was stopped there was no way of knowing who had won and so no one could say for sure which side was right. That was the reason why the videos became popular: if everyone could see a fight, then there was no question about who had won it, or what sort of a job the referees had done. The referees are there to be seen to show fair play and if they can show this on the tape, no one can disagree with the evidence.

THE BEGINNING ...

The fight itself, what I could see of it, was amazing. I had never seen a bare-knuckle fight before and it was compelling to watch. I'd never seen Dan Rooney before; I'd just heard he was a massive man. The McGinleys, I knew, were a big name, and everyone was a little wary of them. A crowd of maybe four hundred showed up, and they sat on the roofs of the houses, on the roof of the church, on the roofs of the shops. All the pubs were closed down around the town square. The police were on the outskirts, but made no attempt to move this crowd because there were too many. McGinley was an entertainer; each day he was on the back of the jeeps, on the back of the lorries, singing songs, while he was waiting for Rooney to turn up.

I watched, not expecting to ever do bare-knuckle fighting myself, but with the training I'd had I was studying the fight as a boxer would do. There's a difference between a fighter and a boxer. One man might be a rough guy, ready for some rough and tumble, then you get this other guy that uses his head, uses his boxing training, making sure his opponent comes nowhere near him. Rooney was a great fighting man but I didn't see as much boxing skill in him as in McGinley.

I had hit someone with my bare fists, in a pub fight that I hadn't looked for. I was in the Clayton Arms in Peckham in a group along with my wife Theresa. One of the Bronx Joyces, David, known as Bushes David, insulted Theresa and pushed her to the ground. I hit him immediately, in the head. It was the first and only time I've had a pub scuffle. I didn't feel good about it at all. Bushes David hit me back and we went outside, but when I put my hands up he let fly, and he was wearing a big ring – traditionally travelling men wear big saddle buckle rings – which caught me under the eye. 'Take that ring off and fight me fair,' I said, but at that moment the police turned up and arrested us both.

The next morning we were released. As soon as I got back to the site I spoke to one of Bushes David's relatives and said, 'I want to fight Bushes for that insult,' but word came back to me that he didn't want to fight as he had only done what he'd done when he was drunk, and he didn't remember pushing Theresa over.

I didn't want to get a reputation as a pub bully, hitting people who said and did things I didn't like. Most of the time, when the following morning I approached the person who'd insulted me, he'd apologise anyway. An apology then was acceptable to me, and I was the bigger person for accepting it. I liked to think I practised what I preached.

My son Hughie was born, like his brother before him, in Guy's Hospital, and when he was three days old, on 7 March 1992, he and his mother came home. I was outside my caravan, cleaning up and busying myself, when Brian Joyce pulled up in his van. 'Are you coming down the pub, James?' He wanted me to join him to celebrate Hughie's arrival at home. 'Curly Paddy's there already,' he said, then went on to list the other members of the families – his and mine – who were there. Brian Joyce and I were drinking pals. There had been arguments between the Joyces and the Quinn McDonaghs way back, but they meant nothing to the two of us – as well as to most of the rest of our families – and hadn't for many years. I replied, 'My wife's only had the kid three days ago. I'm going to stay at home, but if I change my mind I'll follow yous down.' In the end I stayed home with Theresa.

It started off as a normal Saturday night. When they left the pub, Brian Joyce was going to give some people, including my brother and a number of others, a lift back to their caravan site in his van. Neither Brian nor Paddy was involved in what happened next. An argument broke out between two families in the back of the van, and Brian pulled into the site, opened the doors and let everyone out. A fight broke out and Brian tried to break it up but then he got entangled in the argument. The quarrel spread to involve my brother Paddy, a knife was produced and Brian was stabbed.

I didn't know anything about what had happened as I was living a couple of miles away from that site. At about quarter to one in the morning my phone rang. 'James, you've got to come now. There's a man stabbed here. Curly Paddy's in trouble. Hurry.' I was able to leave Theresa and the new baby as my younger sister was staying a few days with us to help Theresa with the boys. I hurriedly dressed and jumped into the car, and took off up the Old Kent Road, driving fast – too fast as far as the police car that pulled me over was concerned. 'What's your hurry?' the policeman said. 'There's an argument going down on the caravan site down the road,' I told him. 'I believe someone's injured. I need to go down there.' I was explaining my speed to him when an ambulance came racing towards us, lights flashing and sirens clanging. I looked at it as it sped past. I didn't know it then but inside was Brian Joyce, on his way to hospital.

'Sir, if there's an incident at the site, you won't help matters now that the police are there. I suggest you go home and wait by the phone instead,' said the policeman. I didn't argue as there was enough chaos going on already and did as he suggested. As soon as I got home I thought of ringing the hospital, as the ambulance racing past had made me think the worst. It took me a while to get someone to talk to me as they didn't want to pass the information on over the phone, but I was able to convince the nurse I was desperate – because I was – and she said, 'Sir, I'm sorry to tell you, but Mr Joyce passed away on his way to hospital. We tried to revive him but there was nothing we could do. I'm sorry, sir, to have to tell you this.'

It was a shock. I'd just been talking to him that very afternoon, and now he was dead. My hand shook as I put the phone down, and I shoved my face into my hands. The next moments were a blur, and it was a while before I could think clearly again. This was serious. A man had been killed, killed on a site where my people lived, and it didn't look good, regardless of who had done it. At the same time I was living in a trailer surrounded by this man's people, with his nephews, his sisters, his brothers, they were all living next to me and I was the only Quinn on the site. My brain seemed to weigh heavily on me. I felt ill trying to think about Brian, and it was a struggle to think clearly at all. I lay awake late into the night, finding it hard to understand what had happened.

The next morning I was still in a daze. A few people were arrested, my brother and two or three more, but I still didn't know what was happening back on the other site. The caravans we were living in were overlooked by a police station which backed onto the site. Any officer who wanted could look out of the window and see just about everything that went on there, but that morning I didn't even think about whether or not they were keeping an eye on us. Until, that is, a policeman appeared and said, 'I'm looking for James Quinn.' 'I'm here,' I replied, and felt myself under the watchful gaze of twenty people. 'We have your brother Paddy locked up, and he wants to know you're OK,' he told me. 'Oh shit,' I said. Around me everyone started looking at each other, and I could see them thinking it through. Do you know what ...? Why would Paddy ask about him ...? He must have been involved in this thing ...

I stepped forward to speak with the officer, saying, 'Look, can we talk in private?' 'Of course,' he replied. Inside my trailer he told me, 'At this stage we haven't brought charges against your brother Paddy. He's been helping us by answering questions regarding this incident.' I almost winced at this last word: Brian Joyce's life – his death – Curly Paddy's freedom – was now an *incident*.

'Right,' I said, and the policeman added, 'He just wants to make sure you're OK. Will you be OK in the site?' I said, 'That depends on you. Is he going to be charged or not going to be charged or ... is he ... did he do this or not?'

The policeman shuffled. 'I can't answer that. I can tell you that he hasn't admitted anything. We're still trying to work out what happened. Before we continued questioning him, though, he did ask that someone come here and find out about your safety.' He gestured at the police station behind us. 'He's fairly worried about you and your family.'

'Can I come in and see him?' I asked. If Paddy was worried about my safety, then I needed to know why.

'You might have to wait until we've finished questioning him,' the officer said, 'but if you don't mind sitting there till we're done then, yes, come in and you can see him.' He seemed very concerned about my situation – which, to be honest, I'd only just noticed, and it made me more tense than ever. I was there on the site with Brian Joyce's nephews, cousins, some other Joyces that were related to me, and they were gathered outside the caravans, staring across at mine, silent. I knew I wasn't going to be able to stay there much longer. I was afraid.

I sat in the station for a while before they brought Paddy out of one of the cells and into a room where I could talk to him. I was still so confused by everything that I didn't take in anything of my surroundings, I just went from a chair in a corridor to the small room where my brother sat. I knew I felt awful but Paddy looked far, far worse, like some part of him had left his body.

'Paddy, what's going on?' I asked him.

He looked down and said, slowly and quietly, 'I don't want anyone else blamed for this, James. I done it. It was a mistake. I was drunk, I didn't mean it to happen. I'm feeling very bad about things.' I sat, stunned. Paddy took a deep breath. 'I'd rather you get out of the camp,' he said. 'Get our family together and go somewhere safe, please. Look after them, James.'

I spoke to the policeman from earlier on, who'd waited outside. I realised now why he was spending so much time with me; they didn't want any more trouble on their patch. 'Are you OK down there?' he asked. 'Will they leave you alone?'

I thought about this. 'The baby's only three days old, I'm sure nothing will happen.' I hoped not anyway. 'We need to move on, but I can't go now as the lights aren't working on the back of the caravan, so I can't take it out at night. I can get away in the morning.' The policeman said, 'We'll keep an eye on you overnight,' and sure enough when I got back to my trailer I could see they'd opened a window in an office over-looking the site and put someone by the window to keep a close watch on us overnight.

The next morning I hooked up the trailer and drove down to the camp where the fatality had happened, and where the rest of my family were also ready to leave with their trailers. As I pulled up outside the camp I could see a large gathering of the Joyces at the other end of the site. The local lads – the Bronx Joyces – had met up with others who'd come over from Ireland, Big Joe Joyce among them.

We decided there and then to get far out of London, for our own safety. It would have been suicide if we'd stayed. When someone dies like that within the traveller community, there'll be a large group coming together, meeting in the pub, the drink will flow, and who knows what will happen then. We were worried they'd want to retaliate in some way, that they'd come down to where we were living. I had a new baby and I couldn't risk that.

We headed to Wales. The next few days were awful, dark days. What happened that night should never have happened, a drunken argument went wrong and it led to a death. Brian Joyce's people of course felt very bad, they felt very hurt, they'd lost a loved one, but they couldn't know how bad we felt. We were in bits, not just for ourselves but for them and for what they'd lost – Brian Joyce had left a young family behind. I'd no argument with the man, I respected him, we'd worked together on building sites, I used to go drinking with him. He was a cousin. He was a genuine person and I liked him, and it was a sad situation for everyone; we were devastated for a long time.

We went round and round this in our heads on that drive down to Wales. My mother and father were both in shock over Paddy being in prison, so the rest of us tried to support them as well. We didn't know where we were going – we just wanted to be as far away from London as we could. We travelled in a group; my mother and father, Paddy's wife Kathleen, my sister Bridgie, my uncle Thomas, Jimmy Gaffney and his wife, and me with my family and newborn son.

We buried in ourselves in Wales and stayed there for the next few months; we didn't go back over to Ireland until the end of September, when we returned to Dundalk. Paddy pleaded guilty to manslaughter and was sentenced to three years in jail. This only made things harder; we were pleased that Paddy hadn't been put inside for longer but the Joyces felt he should have been handed down a life sentence. I can understand why they felt the way they did but I was just happy to know when I would next see my brother.

We heard a lot of threats were made towards us Quinn McDonaghs then. There was a lot of talk about people wanting to fight us, to even kill members of the family. I thought that staying away from London or anywhere the Joyces might be would allow things to calm down a little. All of us – we were four families travelling together – were worried about what the Joyces would do, and we were living in fear in Wales. We were very isolated, with no heating, no hot water, no toilet, no amenities at all, and every time there was a knock on the door we'd flinch, not certain who it was or what was going to happen when we opened it.

When we moved into a new area, the local bobbies would pop down and introduce themselves. Usually we could see right away that they didn't have a problem with us. They'd say, 'How are you? My name is PC Jones and this is PC Smith. What's your name, where are you from?' It was a gentle way of letting us know that they'd got their eyes on us. 'You're here for a few days, are you? When are you thinking of moving on, lads?' We always told them the same thing: that we were just heading down towards the boat back to Ireland. We never told them from which port we were planning to leave, so that gave us the option of driving off either south or north (to Pembroke Dock, Fishguard or Holyhead) as we never wanted to tell anyone, even the police, exactly where we might be going next. We'd say that we were aiming to be on the ferry 'next Monday or Tuesday'. The police would relax when they knew we were leaving: 'All right, stay until next week then,' but when they came back, our plans would have changed. 'We're on next week's boat,' we'd claim, or something like that, and then we'd go on to another area. So for those months we moved around Wales, trying not to get pinned down in any one place and taking only casual jobs.

In the middle of all of this I was called by Seamus Keene, my old boss. 'James, how are you?' I mumbled something in reply. 'I heard what's been going on,' he said. 'Are you OK? And your family?' That was considerate of him, I thought. 'Yes, Seamus, thanks, I'm grand. We're all OK. Thanks for asking.' There was a sigh down the line. 'James, we have a tax problem.' Oh no, I didn't need anything else right now. 'I need your bank details, James. I lost them and you might have to pay a little bit of tax that we've overlooked.' By my silence he could tell I wasn't best pleased. 'I understand it's not a good time, I know there's something going on, and I shouldn't be bothering you at a time like this, but I need your bank numbers straight away.' I said, 'Seamus, I'll give them to you but I don't have the details in front of me now.' He was quick to come back, 'James, there's no need to worry about this, I'll take care of any tax payment if there really is one due. I just need your details for our records or they'll think I'm doing something with the books and go through everything.' I saw what he was after, so I fished out my bank card and read out the details to him.

A couple of days later I went into my bank. I reckoned I might have a hundred quid in there, so I thought I'd check the amount and then withdraw what I had to and no more. The girl at the till handed me a slip which said I had over £3,000 in my account. What? I asked her to check again. It was correct.

I went out the bank and rang Seamus right away. 'What's all this, Seamus?' He said, 'James, I thought you wouldn't have accepted the money if I'd said I was going to give you a few quid. I just wanted to give you that, to make sure you're looked after right now.' I didn't know what to say. He was a good friend.

The death of Brian Joyce reignited the feud between the Quinn McDonaghs and the Joyces, as they wanted revenge. The feud with the Joyces, and the Nevins, went back to a long time before I was born. Every now and again it would flare up; my uncle Anthony, my mother's brother, fought Big Joe Joyce back when they were young, in a pub. No one can be sure who won that one. The barman in the pub said, 'The young blond fellow won it,' meaning my uncle. Someone else would say Big Joe did. The last time there was a fight between our families was in 1975, when about twenty people were arrested at my grandfather's house, a mixture of all three of the clans, and sixteen of them went to prison. I don't know – because I was too young at the time – why they were fighting. Anyway they shared prison cells and when they got out they were friends again.

They should have been friends because they were all related. Patsy Joyce – many generations ago – married one of the Quinn women and this went on down the years: brother and sister would marry brother and sister until there were so many cousins that they were all connected. Brian Joyce's father and my grandfather were double first cousins. That's how close we all were.

So we didn't know for certain what the Joyces felt about us at that time; we knew they hated us, but just not how badly. When, in the old days, clans were feuding, to issue a challenge to fight one of the clans would mean getting someone neutral to travel the twenty or thirty miles over to the camp where the other fellow was, and issue the challenge to his face. When video cameras came in, the taunts were taped and the challenges sent over to the family to watch. Then it became DVDs; now it's mobile phones and YouTube.

We'd heard nothing from the Joyces, so, when Edward Hendry, a very good friend of my father's, died eighteen months later, we thought it was safe to go to his funeral in Derby. We decided then – out of our own stupidity – to travel back down to London for a drinking session with the Joyces. We had no argument with them, or so we thought, as with Paddy being in jail we thought it was all resolved. We headed to the Clayton Arms, about two hundred yards from where I'd been living when Brian Joyce died. We met my cousins there and we were standing and talking to them for most of the evening. While we were there I noticed a little fellow, someone I knew to be a friend of the Bronx Joyces, watching us. When I looked over later he'd gone, and I didn't think anything of it.

When it came to closing time, our small group decided to leave; the site where we'd be put up for the night was only a short walk away and we had to go right past the police station to get there. I was first out of the door, and as I stepped out of the pub I happened to glance to my left.

Coming towards us was a group of about thirty of the Bronx Joyces, waving swords, knives, hammers, slash hooks, bill hooks – anything sharp they could get their hands on – and when they saw I had caught sight of them they started running towards us.

My father came out behind me and I swore, grabbed his arm, and started to take off. My cousin Mickey and his brother Joe yelled, 'James, you run on, they're going to kill you. We'll look after your dad – they won't hurt him because he's older,' and pushed me ahead. By now I was halfway across the road and I dropped my grip and ran ahead. I looked over my shoulder and the Bronxes were closing in, shouting and jeering at us, and I suddenly thought, why would they be all right to my father? But I couldn't stop, not now, I couldn't stand up to that many men all armed with sharp weapons. I ran down into the site and into my sister's caravan, shouted to her to get back from the door, then turned to slam it shut and lock it. Two or three of the Joyces had caught up with me and banged on the door but they went away quickly – being so close to a police station had its advantages. I waited till it was quiet, then opened the door to go and look for my father.

There was no sign of any crowd now: they'd disappeared as soon as they'd first shown up. Mickey and Joe had protected my father but when I reached him I could see blood coming down onto his shirt; he'd been slashed around the neck, a twenty-inch scar from the bottom of his ear down to the top of the opposite shoulder. We phoned for an ambulance and luckily one came quickly as my father was losing a lot of blood.

Of course the police rapidly put in an appearance. My father said he didn't know who they were and that he had been too drunk to have any idea of why he'd been attacked.

Now the feud was well and truly alive again.

5

NEVINS I:
DITSY NEVIN

Nineteen ninety-three, we hoped, would be a better year for the Quinn McDonaghs. In the summer my younger sister, Mary, got married, to Cowboy John Joe – a cousin, of course. A lot of cousins, even Joyces, as well as Nevins, were at the wedding on 23 June. It was a warm summer's day and a lot of drinking went on. It didn't take long for a scuffle to break out once the drinking was underway. Ditsy Nevin pushed his way into the middle of the floor, roaring at everyone. He pulled off his shirt and slapped himself on the chest. 'I will ...' he shouted out, slurring, 'I will fight anyone – anyone in this room.'

Christy 'Ditsy' Nevin was a fighting man. Like Big Joe Joyce, he liked a fight and he liked to talk about fighting. His fighting days, though, were a long way behind him now, as he was about 37, and he had been drinking. But he was disturbing my sister's wedding and he had made me cross. Ditsy was acting like a bully and that was the one thing I didn't like. I looked around and there was no one, no one going out to face him, to tell him to behave himself and to take up his challenge. I was still a scrawny thing, built like a dandelion, and I'd not fought anyone in a challenge like this, but someone needed to stop him, and if no one else was going to have a go, then it looked like it was going to be me. I didn't for a moment think of the consequences – of him hurting me, of my wife and my mother being unhappy to see me fighting – I just did what felt right to me.

I moved out into the space Ditsy had formed around himself as he whirled about, punching the air, and said, 'Ditsy, I'll go out. I'll have a fight with you if that's what you want.'

Everyone else looked round and Ditsy, who was looking the other way, turned to face me, raising his fists as he did so. My uncle Anthony stepped in quickly and said, 'All right, James, if that's what you want. Let's take it outside. And Ditsy, drop the rings.' Ditsy looked at his hands and he had some big traveller's rings on his fingers, so he pulled them off and handed them to one of his nephews standing beside him.

We went outside the hall. All the men came after us, boys pushing their ways between their legs to watch. Everyone stood in a loose circle around us as Ditsy and I faced each other. Uncle Anthony said, 'Right, on you go.' I hadn't taken my shirt off, but I'd rolled up my sleeves. I stood back in the proper stance, got my balance right, and raised my hands.

Ditsy lunged forward, slicing at my face with his left. The momentum carried him past me as I stepped out to my right, and he left himself wide open. With my one and only punch, I hit him on the side of the head, he went down and out immediately, and the fight was over.

There were a few cheers from the people he'd annoyed with his behaviour, and a few hands patting me on the shoulders, but that was it. His sons and nephews looked a bit shocked but my uncle Anthony said, 'Come on, lads, help me with your father,' and they picked Ditsy up and carried him to his van. I suppose they'd been brought up with all the stories of Ditsy's fighting skills and had never expected to see him beaten so easily. I watched as the seven or eight of them drove off, and then went back to my sister's party.

The Nevins didn't go home, though. They drove to my uncle Anthony's house, broke in through the windows, and smashed everything inside. What they couldn't break they ripped apart – the place was demolished. My uncle hadn't done anything to them, had made sure they'd left the place safely, had helped them take their father away, and this is what they did. I couldn't understand why they'd done what they did, but then I heard later what the Nevins told others about Ditsy's fight.

'It was a stupid thing, he was drunk,' said Spike Nevin. But then he added that we – the Quinn McDonaghs – took Ditsy outside 'and gave him a bit of a hiding', which was just a lie.

'Twenty big young fellas beat me up,' said Ditsy. 'Big fellas, 19 years of age.'

Ditsy had a thing against the Quinn McDonaghs, dating back many years. He said his father had been beaten up at a horse fair 'by fifty men', among them Quinn McDonaghs. Their caravan was, he claimed, turned over while Ditsy, then a young boy, was inside it, along with four or five of his younger brothers and sisters. 'I never forgot that,' he said.

I didn't feel good about hitting Ditsy. Seeing someone goading people like he had been had kicked up a reaction in me I wasn't used to: the desire to stop him in the way he was used to, that is, to hit him. That wasn't me, that wasn't what I usually did, but somehow Ditsy had provoked this reaction in me and I had no outlet for it other than to do what he wanted – to take him on. I think it was a defensive feeling, because he was acting out at my sister's wedding, at her party, and it was not right of him to make such a spectacle there when it should have been a happy day for her. The feeling that welled up in me was a bad one. It wasn't evil – but I was surprised to feel it inside myself. I suppose without it I wouldn't have been able to fight him, but it wasn't like any feeling I'd had in the boxing ring when I'd sparred with people, or even when I'd had the fight in the pub. This was a new feeling to me, an aggression that felt hot and burning inside. I suppose I needed to have this killer instinct, otherwise I'd have been better off ballet dancing.

I was a bit surprised at how easily Ditsy had gone down. From his reputation, I thought he would have landed a few punches on me.

Then a week later Ditsy called my uncle Anthony and told him, 'I want to fight that bastard for hitting me and knocking me down with his first punch. I wasn't ready for him – I was drunk.' So one of my cousins called me and said, 'James, Ditsy wants to fight you again over that punch at the wedding. The man was drunk. Have a fight with him, you owe him a fight, but you be careful, he can fight.' No one expected me to fight; no one had ever seen me fight. I'd boxed in the ring but that was years ago and no one had any idea that I could fight someone like Ditsy, who was an experienced fighter. The people around me were saying things like, 'No, you can't, James. You can just tell the man you won't fight. The man's a champion, he's going to get you.' But what did I have to lose? I wasn't a fighting man, I wasn't classed as a fighting man, I'd never had a fight, whereas Ditsy was a bare-knuckle boxer. This would be my first fight but he would have had – well, I didn't know how many fights he'd had. I expected his people were telling him I'd be too scared to fight and he needn't worry about me. Maybe it surprised him a bit when I said, 'Aye, I'll fight the man.'

Ditsy thinks this happened differently, that he was told that 'if I didn't fight James they'd come back and kill me and burn the caravan'. I don't know where he got that idea from – why would I want to fight him? No good could come out of it, I knew that. All I know is Ditsy was asked to let it go but he said, 'No, I was made a show of. I want to fight.'

So the challenge was thrown down for a fight three or four days later. I didn't do anything to prepare for the fight at all, I just carried on with my normal life, and that meant I carried on going to the pub – although I cut down on my drinking while I was there. I was having a glass of Coke in a pub in Dundalk the night before the fight when one of my cousins came over to me. 'James, are you sure you want to fight this man?' he asked. 'It's just you ... you don't look nervous.' I looked up at him in surprise. 'Nervous about what? I don't know what to be nervous about. If I lose, I lose.' I was not expecting to win. I'd had no expectation of going out and beating the man. After all, he had a reputation, he was supposed to be a fearsome fighting man, and I was a scrawny thirteen and a half stone nothing. No one knew me, no one ever heard of me, I was nobody. I was somebody to my family, but that was it. What did I have to be nervous about?

The next morning I realised what my cousin was talking about. Paddy, who was wrapping my bandages on my hands, said to me, 'All right, James? Butterflies in your stomach?' I rubbed my stomach with my free hand. 'I tell you what, Paddy, never mind butterflies, it's like seagulls in there!'

This was the first time I'd ever felt like this; it was as if I was about to be sick. When I walked out to where we were going to fight, there were about two hundred and fifty travellers standing around, waiting for the fight to start. A few loud cheers came out, along with some boos. All those eyes were on me and I wasn't sure if I could take that attention. I hadn't looked for it – this was all Ditsy's doing. Paddy gripped my shoulder tightly and I said to him, 'I didn't want this, you know. This is going to get me nowhere.' He barked into my ear, 'The fight's on now, James. Beat him.'

There were going to be eight fights in all that day between Quinn McDonagh men and Nevin men, and Ditsy fighting me was the first. He came over and the referees explained the rules of the fair fight: no biting, no head-butting, no holding, no breaks, no dirty punches. I said to Ditsy, 'Look, you shouldn't have done this, you shouldn't have sent for this fight.' He replied, 'I don't give a fuck what you think. Now let's get at it.'

'Go to it now, lads,' said one of the referees, and we both moved to fight.

At the start I hung back a bit. I wanted to see what Ditsy could do, and I wasn't going to go charging in there, hoping to land one on him, only to get a severe hammering myself, so I danced about a bit, stayed away from him as best as I could. I kept moving my head about in a different direction from my body, weaving about a bit, leaning back if he swung an arm out at me. When I could, I would step a bit to the side and try to get him on the face. Nothing too much at this stage: I just wanted to let him know I could hit him if I wanted to, and to stop the referee from getting on my back, as he urged us to get into it together and fight.

I didn't hear anything from the crowd the whole time I was facing Ditsy, and they might as well not have been there. I was concentrating so hard on the fight that I blocked everything else out, except for the voice of the referee, because I was supposed to hear him, because I was supposed to obey the rules and the laws of bare-knuckle boxing. I hadn't planned to do that, but as soon as I started fighting that's what happened. The same with my nerves; as soon as we started, the butterflies in my stomach disappeared.

Maybe a minute or two passed – I had no way of judging the time – but after a bit I realised that Ditsy was not reaching me with his punches – I was fending them off with my left – but that when I jabbed him with my right I was making contact every time. I had long arms, maybe that was it, I was younger, I was fitter, I don't know what it was, but I had more luck hitting him than he had getting at me. Fighting without gloves meant his skin marked more quickly (probably mine too under the bandages) and I saw that each time I hit him he'd get a graze or a scratch.

Every time Ditsy threw a punch, I was four or five inches away from him. I was too quick for him and went back a step so he couldn't hit me, every time. And when I went in, I got him. He wasn't fit enough to get back. This isn't right, I thought to myself. He should be hitting me, he's the fighting man. I thought maybe he would wait till I left myself open and then hit me hard, that he was taking my punches to fool me. Well, if he's going to trick me, put me down, then until he does so I'll do my best to mark him, let everyone see I put up a fight, so if I lose at least I can say I cut him.

A couple of minutes later, after we'd danced around again, I realised that Ditsy wasn't going to be doing anything to me after all. He wasn't capable of hurting me. Fuck this, I thought, I'm going to walk this fight. I was feeling good and fit, so I decided to push him a bit harder and see what I could do. I went forward, he recoiled back, I feinted with my left, and then let fly with a hard punch from my right. His hands went up to protect his face and I let go with both hands at the sides of his head and his chest.

Ditsy then went backwards, put his arms down, turned to the referee, said, 'I'm done,' and that was it. The crowd started clapping and I looked round, shocked. That was it? I'd beaten him? That was the fight? I don't think he'd even landed a blow on me that I felt at the end of the fight. We'd only been at it for maybe six minutes, maybe seven. I didn't know that, I had no sense of time then, I was concentrating so hard. It could have been moments, it could have been hours. I wouldn't have known the difference.

Suddenly from among the crowd a man came out with a white towel that he chucked at Ditsy; one of the women had come out of the caravans and handed it to him to pass on. When Ditsy wiped his face and body the towel came away covered in blood, and I was surprised. I hadn't hit him hard, not really, but his skin was scratched and grazed in enough places that he turned the towel red like that.

After I fought Ditsy, Cowboy Davey fought Patrick in the second fight; then Martin Anthony, my uncle Anthony's son, won his fight against one of the young Nevins. Paddy fought Ditsy's brother Joe, and Paddy won. Cousin Sammy fought Sadler Reilly, and won. Cowboys Martin won his fight on the day, Cowboy Hughie fought Ditsy's Ollie and lost, but then Hughie wasn't a boxer and Ollie was. (Why we call Martin 'Cowboys Martin', and another cousin 'Cowboys Michael', rather than 'Cowboy', I don't know.)

In the end we won the day, with the scoreboard showing all wins for the Quinn McDonaghs apart from one for the Nevins. We went back to Dundalk and had a big booze-up, and I was the main man for the evening – the first time – and I liked it.

Ditsy said later he fought me with 'three fractured ribs', which he said he'd got when he'd been attacked outside the wedding a few days before. I can't say as I noticed that then. He also said that I was no good as a fighter because if he'd been in my position, fighting someone injured like that, he'd have knocked me out sooner. (I find this often happens: a man who's lost a fight will find all sorts of things to say that deflect attention from that one undeniable fact: that he lost the fight against a better man.)

I didn't get a lot of time to myself that evening, as everyone wanted to buy me a drink and share in the memory of the fight, but when I was alone I thought about what had happened. So much had suddenly changed. I had never been in a fight before, at least not one that counted or which lasted beyond a few quick slaps. Now I was being cheered and having my health drunk to by dozens and dozens of men. All I'd done was stand in front of someone older than me and hit him in the face with my bare fists. He was probably somewhere else, not feeling too good right now.

Did I feel great about it? No, not really. I didn't feel proud, I didn't feel happy. I didn't want to hurt Ditsy. He was the one who'd asked for the fight, so anything that happened to him was his fault. Once he'd done that I was only doing what he'd asked me to do; the fight had become my job, that was all. Winning the fight became the job – hurting him was not part of that. When I was standing in front of the guy, just before the fight started, I was switched on, I was grand.

But when the referee said, right lads, get at it, keep it clean – then I changed into a different person. When I was looking at Ditsy as I fought him, I genuinely felt that I want to hurt him. I know from seeing the photos people showed me how very angry I looked, and I wasn't faking that to try to scare Ditsy or put him off, but I had no idea at the time that it showed on my face. And when I was alone later that evening, I thought about how that wasn't something I'd put on, that it was me wanting to sink my hand into his head, trying to push it out the other side. Because Ditsy was the man who came looking for this trouble. He asked for this – not me.

Theresa was the only one I didn't have to tell: she knew me well enough to know what I was going through. She knew without me having to say anything that as much as I liked being in the pub, the men singing my name, the drink flowing, she also knew that I wasn't someone who wanted to fight. She knew what success meant to me; that I'd done my family proud, and that was what mattered to me. But she also knew what a great relief had come off my shoulders now that I'd come home safe, not injured in any way. It was as much about not losing as it was about winning. I was just starting to realise this.

Cowboy Davey, Cowboy Hughie and my wife, Theresa. [1971, Mullingar]

My son, JJ, and my brother, Dave, at the caravan site where Brian Joyce was killed. [Peckham, 1992]

My brother, Dave, and father, Jimmy. [Wales, 1992]

My mother, Teresa, holding my son, Hughie, with my brother, Michael, holding my niece, Bridge. [Pyle, Wales, 1992]

Hughie's christening — my mother, me, the priest and Hughie, Theresa and my father. [1992]

Me, Theresa and JJ. [Peckham, 1987]

Theresa and my cousins (Linda, Helen, Julie — all Joyces). [The Spinning Wheel, Dundalk, 1996]

The Quinn, Joyce and Collins clans celebrating together at an Oxford Joyce's Wedding (left to right): Winnie Joyce, Kathleen Collins, Theresa, Tom Collins and Maggie Quinn. [Oxford, Late 1980s]

Hughie, with Davey 'Minor Charge' Quinn behind him,
and Eugene, a cousin. [Dublin, 1998]

Keeping Davey Nevin at distance with the long reach
of my jab during our fight. [2001]

Catching Davey Nevin with a left hook. [2001]

Enjoying a well-deserved holiday, far from the stress of training. [Santa Ponsa, 2001]

My son, Hughie, with my nephew, Jimmy, and me — one of the photos that I managed to save from the fire. [Dunsink Lane, 2001]

Theresa and Hughie. [Dunsink Lane, 2001]

My grandmother, Auld Biddy, holding JJ's James (my grandson and her great, great grandson). Auld Biddy connects us to the other clans — she was a second cousin of Big Joe Joyce, and the aunt of both 'Chaps' Patrick and Ditsy Nevin. The little girl is Chloe (daughter of Cowboy Hughie). [2009]

My parents and siblings (left to right): Michael, Mary, Dave, Maggie, me, Paddy, Bridgie. Front Row: my parents, Jimmy and Teresa. [Dundalk, 2008]

Cowboy Davey, Patrick, D-Boy and me taking a break from a game of pool — I always win ... [2009]

My brother Michael's fight with Paul Joyce, which ended as a draw.
I was proud of Michael, as we all were. [Hemel Hempstead, 2007]

Me and Bobby Gunn, the US Heavyweight Bare-Knuckle Champion.
Who knows what the future holds? [New Jersey, 2009]

6

NEVINS II:
CHAPS PATRICK

Six or seven months later I was out in the fields doing some farm work, picking spuds. There were twenty of us in a field in Dundalk, moving up and down the rows, each working on our own section, plunging our hands into the sticky mud to pick up the potatoes turned up by the tractor. It was only my second day in the field and bending down while on my feet all day made my legs and my back sore. I'd need to stretch myself out every now and again; in a few days' time I'd be used to it but not yet. When I was pushing on my back to ease the pain I heard someone call my name and I looked up to see two of my cousins, Cowboy Davey and Sammy, in the distance walking across the field towards me.

'Not good,' I said to myself. Right away I knew that whatever they were there for couldn't be good news, as they lived a long way from Dundalk and, it being a weekday morning, they hadn't come all the way out here to go drinking with me.

I peered more closely and could see that Cowboy Davey had a piece of paper in his hand. Not good at all.

When they were close enough I said, 'What's up, boys?' The pair of them were stepping heavily in the mud now – they'd not worn shoes for the potato fields – and when they'd waded over to me Davey said, 'Chaps Patrick wants to fight you.' Ah, I thought, understanding now why they'd come and what the piece of paper was. 'For what?' I asked. Davey replied, 'About you beating his cousin Ditsy. He said Ditsy was too old and wasn't fit. He wants to stand up for Ditsy. He's the same age as you, fitter and stronger, which would make the fight a fair fight.' Chaps Patrick certainly was fitter and stronger. 'Right,' I said, and thought for a moment. I looked back at the row of spuds I'd just cleared and the box and a half I'd just picked up, and called over to my neighbour working on the drill next to me. 'Gerry,' I said. 'Come here.' 'What?' he asked. 'Those two boxes of spuds I've picked, you have them, you keep them. I'm off.' And I walked off the field, because I knew that this fight was going to be different and I didn't want to work today. I wanted to think about it.

The three of us walked off the field and sat in my car. 'What's this all about then, boys? When does he want to fight?' Cowboy Davey brought out the piece of paper, which had numbers written on it. 'He wants you to fight him next week, James. If you agree, then he's put a number down here for us to call and agree a day.' I didn't think for a minute, I'm 27 years old. I was thinking, I'm fit enough to face him. I'd beaten Ditsy easily enough, so I thought I could take his cousin too. 'Tell him yes. Say next week will do. Let's get it out of the way.'

I didn't do any training for the fight at all. I relied on who I was, how strong I was, right then. I was still sure of myself. So sure of myself that I even suggested we have a little wager on the fight. We were in the pub a few nights later, talking about the fight, and it came to me. If we're going to do this, I said, if we're going to go somewhere and knock each other about, why not have a little something to show for it at the end? Why not put in £10,000 for the winner?

Chaps Patrick was having none of it. The fight was about respect for his cousin Ditsy, that was it. No purse. So I forgot all about it.

On the morning of the fight, twenty or thirty Quinn McDonaghs gathered at my trailer and, together with my father and brothers, they set out for my grandfather's house in Mullingar. My referee – Patrick McGinley – came to pick me up, and he drove me out to one of the lakes outside Mullingar, Lough Ennell. We stopped in some woods to the side of the water and I got out of the car there. Chaps Patrick was waiting by his car and when I stepped out he pulled off his shirt and I looked at him and I thought, I'm in trouble here. He's a big lad, I knew that already, but he looked strong and fit – stronger and fitter than me – and I had to stop myself from looking at him and patting my own little bulging rabbit's belly. I was drinking too much and hadn't been training at all – I realised that looking at him – but it was too late to think about that now.

I pulled off my shirt and went towards him. We shook hands, the referees told us what rules they expected us to obey, and I put my hands up ready. Here I was, I'd had one fight, and I was being the bare-knuckle boxer as naturally as you like. It didn't feel odd to me to be standing there with my fists up and no gloves on them. It didn't feel wrong, it just felt like I'd forgotten one last bit of kit, that was all.

Chaps Patrick came at me quickly and landed a few on me right away. This wasn't like fighting Ditsy, when I'd been comfortable and in charge right from the start. I was going to have to concentrate if I wasn't going to get hurt here. I had my arms up against my body and my fists tight in front of my face and he thumped the side of my head a couple of times. To keep him away from me, I pushed out my left hand – keeping my right back to cover my chin – and waved it about in front of him, to block his view of me and to stop him reaching me as easily as he had done in the opening moments.

Without planning to, just using it to defend myself, I'd brought back the 'fishing pole' that I'd used at the Darndale Boxing Club in Dublin and that my trainer had then tried to get rid of from my fighting. I needed to because Chaps Patrick was moving about me quickly and jumping on his toes to get round to have a clear shot at me. I wasn't nearly as fit as I'd been when fighting Ditsy and I needed to keep my mind sharp if I was going to survive this without getting badly hurt. This time it worked a treat. I felt protected with my left arm out in front of me, my right hand back ready to snap out at him.

We kept jabbing away at each other like that. He landed no serious punches on me but I didn't manage to mark him at all. The referees kept on urging us on to fight, not to hang back. I knew things were going wrong for me when I needed to get my second wind as Chaps Patrick had almost exhausted me. We'd been fighting for almost twenty minutes and I realised I had no idea what to do next. I had to do something soon or I was going to lose the fight – that was starting to become clear to me, and I didn't like it.

I was uneducated as a street-fighter. As a boxer I knew what I was doing, but not out here in the open air. No breaks meant I had to concentrate – one moment of not watching him and I'd be on my arse – and I had to get some more energy in me. I remembered what I'd been taught in the club. 'If you're tired, step back, pretend you're still in the fight. Breathe. Breathe through your nose, blow it out your mouth slowly, you don't want your opponent to think you're spent. Take deep breaths. All the time pretend you're still active. Keep your guard up. Pretend you're still fighting while you breathe.'

This I did, getting myself into a defensive stance, but all the time Chaps Patrick was catching me, hurting me. Keeping my hands up protected my face as he thudded his fists into my arms and to the side of my head, catching my ears painfully as he did so. But still I hadn't managed to leave a mark on him, nothing.

I wasn't winning, I felt I was just going to drop dead of exhaustion, and it was only half an hour. I was nowhere near fit enough, and was moving slowly and heavily. I needed to get more air into me. I had to keep in this position for a while, trying to breathe, thinking of what I could do to win the fight – because if nothing changed then I was down and out. For about five minutes I held my position, in a defensive system, and protected my jaw – a good punch to the chin would have sent a signal right through me and my brain would have told my legs to fold and get away from more pain by sitting down. If he had hit me, it would have been a hard punch to take because he was solid and strong. A punch to the stomach would have completely winded me and as I had no wind in me anyway I would have had to give up. I slid my arms down whenever he came at my chest and stomach. Otherwise I kept them up around my jaw – with nine out of ten punches he only connected with my arms, but the ones getting through to my head were hurting me.

The referees urged me on to fight. They were wise enough to see what I was up to, and they tried to get me to fight back because otherwise they were going to have to ask me if I wanted to offer Chaps Patrick my hand. I moved about as much as I could, so they wouldn't think I was quitting: switching sides, pushing my left arm out to keep him away if I could hold it up for long enough. Gradually I could feel the energy coming back into me; the breathing allowed me to reload myself, and switching about seemed to bother him. I could feel he was tiring too, that the punches that connected with my arms were not as powerful as before but that he'd worn himself out flailing away at me, and I bet to myself that he wished he could take a break.

As I was moving about, taking some air in, holding off his punches as best I could, I heard a voice shouting out at me. I'd managed to block out the noise around me and tried to pay attention only to the referee's voice, but there was something about the tone that cut through the wall I'd put up around myself.

It was Big Joe Joyce. 'Well, young Quinn, I bet that ten thousand doesn't look so good to you right now,' he jeered.

He'd been arguing with my uncle Anthony. The two of them were our seconds: my uncle was there for me, Big Joe was there for Chaps Patrick, and they didn't like each other. They'd fought each other years back and had been arguing on the sidelines until that moment when Big Joe popped up with his sarcastic remark.

When the fight was over I could point to this moment as the moment I decided I was not going to lose, I was going to win. If Joe had asked me, I'd have said, 'Thanks, Joe, you helped me win this fight.' Big Joe and his sons and cousins and the Nevins between themselves had created this character of a fighter that they thought I was, and it was this moment, when Joe spoke like that, that the fighter came out in me. Up till then I'd been on my way out of the fight, but when Joe said that it was like he opened up something in my mind. He should have kept his mouth closed, he was only an observer, the fight had fuck all to do with him. But a determination, a fierceness, came out in me. Joe's snide remark pushed the adrenalin back into me and I moved in and started punching Chaps Patrick back.

I bent the elbow of my left arm slightly so that Chaps Patrick would think I was at full stretch and lean a little towards me as he came in – only I'd then jab forward and catch him. I shifted over so that I could start using my left to hit him, to get him watching that, then switch quickly over to my right. These were my old boxing tricks and they came back to me now as the energy surged into me. It worked for me and it confused him: he was there watching this long left hovering around his face, then suddenly I'd throw my right.

I turned that fight around within twelve or thirteen minutes. Four or five minutes after Joe spoke, I had Chaps Patrick on the ground with a left hook and cut him badly. I'd split his skin a little, about an inch or so over the eye, and as he rolled on the ground the referee said, 'Are you beat?' He turned round and said, 'No, no, no, I'm only taking a break.' The referee snapped back, 'Get the fuck up, you can't take a break. Are you fighting?' Chaps Patrick heaved himself up, and said, 'I'll fight.' From then on I knew that I'd won the fight. By now I had my second wind, and went for the kill. I followed him because he was back-pedalling. He kept falling down and getting up, and I kept hitting him. I didn't knock him out because I wasn't sinking the punches in the way I wanted to get them in, as he wasn't walking into a punch, he was walking away from it. He went down another four times before we finished.

When he went down the next time, he stumbled back up to his feet and then stuck out his hand to shake mine. 'Are you done?' the referees asked him, and he nodded.

I did something then that I shouldn't have done. I was still pumping full of anger. I hadn't wanted this fight, I didn't want to become some sort of target, so I tried to say to him that now I'd beaten him I didn't want anyone else coming up to try and fight me. The fighting, as far as I was concerned, was over. 'I'm only being fair,' I said. 'As there's cameras here now, I am definitely no good to fight. But ...' – and I clapped Chaps Patrick on the shoulder as I said this – 'I will say one thing: fair play to you. You did the best you could, but no Nevin will ever, ever beat me.'

I didn't say this as a challenge to them. I meant it to be a way of stopping the fighting. Let's have no more of this, is what I thought. I'm done with these challenges. I should have known better. Those words burned into the Nevins and as a result they seethed with resentment towards me for years.

The cameras that had filmed the fight were turned off Chaps Patrick and together we walked down to the lake at the edge of the woods and stepped into the water to wash the mud and blood off us both. I stuck my head into the water for a moment and the thick ears Chaps Patrick had given me throbbed in the cold. I said to him, 'That's over now, Patrick. What was that all about anyway?' and he said, 'It was over Ditsy.' He spat some blood out of his mouth and probed gently at a tooth. 'You beat me fair and square, forget about it. D'you want to go for a pint?' he asked. I thought, why didn't they film this bit? Maybe if all those Quinn McDonaghs, Nevins and Joyces who'd watch this film to see us fighting instead saw us talking about going to the pub afterwards for a drink together, they might not feel they had to fight too.

The films are an important record of the fight, because neither side can have any supporters there. If my supporters had started cheering me on and getting louder than Chaps Patrick's supporters, then the two groups might have ended up fighting each other and the whole thing would have run out of control. It's meant to be a fair fight, not a mass brawl. The only way any of the clans were going to see my fight with Chaps Patrick after we'd fought was via the film. The cameraman filming the fight for the Quinn McDonaghs had got a bit carried away when he was filming, as I discovered when I went back to the site to watch the video with my family. We missed crucial moments in the fight, because the cameraman took his eye away from the viewfinder and watched the moment, pulling the camera back to the fight when whatever had excited him was over. So every now and again we'd be staring at the TV when the picture would suddenly flick down to the back of someone's head, or the ground, and we'd hear excited shouts of 'C'mon, James!' before the camera would flick back up. I sit with the family to watch the fights and I'm always surprised to find that a lot goes on that I don't recall. I must be concentrating so hard on what I'm doing that I blank out a lot of what's going on around me – and maybe also what's just happened. I have to rewind and watch the tape again, wondering, when did I do that much? How did he hit me there? Or thinking, I don't remember that at all.

The Nevins had brought their own cameraman so that they could watch the fight as well – though I'd be very surprised if anyone sat around watching their brother or son or cousin lose a fight. The father's pride would have been dented, and, anyway, no mother likes to see her son fight, win or lose. When he comes back from a fight, she's got to look after her son when he's just been beaten up. Her heart's broken, her son had just lost and let down a couple of hundred people. His wife has to take him home, and he's probably hard to live with for a little while. Anyone who's lost a fight must be a hard person to live with, even for a short length of time. Anyway, most traveller women want to see an end to bare-knuckle boxing, and an end to the feuding that their families are involved in. I suppose it's because traveller women are more religious than the men.

But the feud between our clans worsened. In November 1995 an argument broke out between a group of the Joyces and a few of the Quinn McDonaghs in a pub in Finglas, in Dublin. It was a pub that a lot of travellers would drink in because the landlord welcomed them in the days when it was very hard for a large group of travellers to get served in a pub together. Individually they might be let in, but a group of them would most likely be turned away. Something sparked off the row between the two clans in the pub – I don't know what, I was in Dundalk at the time – and in the fight that broke out Tim Joyce, Brian's brother, was killed. My uncle Davey was convicted of his murder and is serving life. Now when my brother Paddy was convicted of manslaughter he admitted his responsibility. Davey has always said he didn't kill the man. Big Joe Joyce later swore an affidavit that the evidence identifying Davey as the man responsible for Tim Joyce's death was incorrect. Where that will end up, I don't know.

The feud started to grow from there.

7

JOYCES I:
JODY'S JOE JOYCE

A group of travellers had organised a sports event for the kids one weekend at Phoenix Park in Dublin, the idea being that the kids should bring their dads along for a bit of fun. There'd be some matches between the different groups and we'd all have a kickabout. It wasn't supposed to mean anything other than that. We Quinns fielded a team, along with the Joyces, Wards and Nevins, who all had teams out there. Not enough Quinns turned up to make a team, so one of the Collinses joined us as well. We played half an hour a side.

I played but, as I mentioned, I'm the worst footballer there is. However, I'm big, so I was stuck in defence and told to stand there and not let anyone get past me. I was so bad at the game that I was there just for my brute force. The best I could do was commit fouls, trip people up as they ran towards me, block them off, anything I could.

We were playing the Joyces, and I can't remember who was winning but Jody's Joe was putting in some tackles that one or two of his opponents took exception to, so they would swing a fist at him. In our match an argument broke out between him and one of my cousins and it spilled over into the Quinns and Joyces watching on the sidelines. My uncle Anthony was there with his son D-Boy. D-Boy was a boxer, but he'd broken his foot and was there on crutches. When the argument blew up, Jody Joyce pulled a knife on my uncle Anthony and went to stab him with it. Anthony pulled out one of D-Boy's crutches and started poking away at him with it, keeping him and the knife away. By this time I had raced over and grabbed the other crutch – I don't know how D-Boy stayed upright – and whacked Jody Joyce hard in the ribs, to make him drop the knife. He was so winded by the blow he dropped to the ground, along with the knife.

It was all over so quickly. Other travellers raced over, some Guards turned up, we were all separated, and that was the end of the tournament. I went home and thought no more about it, until the day a few months later when I got a call from my sister back in England. She was married to one of the Joyces and so the message was passed through her: 'Jody's Joe wants to fight you,' she said. 'What? Why?' I said. 'Over you hitting Jody Joyce with that crutch.' 'Oh, right. When does he want to fight?' 'In a week, two weeks, whenever.' I thought back to my last fights. Not so much those two fights with Ditsy Nevin, because I was younger then; more about the fight with Chaps Patrick and how his strength and fitness had nearly done for me. So I told my sister, 'No. I'm not going to fight until I know I'm ready,' because I would have to do some training for this fight. I wanted to be ready, because I knew that if I lost, I'd have no excuse. If I wasn't ready for him, and fought him and lost, then I'd always think to myself, what if I'd been fitter, or faster, or stronger? That would have eaten me up, and I couldn't risk that.

This would be the first Joyce fight I had, so it was a good idea to see how serious they were about it. I rang them to see if I could put some money on the fight, but the Joyces said no. 'He just wants to fight you, with not one penny going on the fight, because of what you've done to his cousin.' They were right because I had done the wrong thing in Phoenix Park. Knocking the knife out of the old man's hand was one thing, but I shouldn't have knocked the wind out of his body, I shouldn't have lifted a crutch and hit him with it. At the end of the day the old man didn't deserve it, so I had to show this young fellow respect by accepting the challenge.

I knew I had to get into training for this fight because this time I would be fighting an all-Ireland champion. I had a height and weight advantage over Jody's Joe, but that's not enough – as I'd discovered – in a street-fighter. I needed to be fast, I needed to improve my technique, I needed to have stamina, and I needed to use my brain more. I would have to think carefully about the fight – what I was going to do, what he was going to do, and what I had to do if my plans started to go wrong. In a ring you have breaks and your trainer will tell you what to do next if you need help. But as a street-fighter, once I was out there in front of Jody's Joe I'd be on my own. I had to make my plans ahead of the fight, and be as well prepared as I could be.

Jody's Joe had fought a few fights – one in England too – and he'd fought a cousin of mine, so I knew a little about him and what I'd have to be ready for. I went into the Gym, in Avenue Road, Dundalk, run by Clive McGuinness, and told him what I was up against, and what I needed to do in the next two weeks to be ready. Clive was someone I'd been drinking with, so it wasn't much of a surprise to him when I said I was going to be fighting soon and needed to train for it. I was honest about what I needed his help with, and he asked me, 'What type of training are you hoping to do?' I'd already thought about this and so I said, 'A lot of boxing training, a lot of fitness training, and a lot of weight training, because I want to build myself up. I want to start right away, and I hate running, so I'll have to go for a light jog first, before I start on anything else, because if I don't do it, then I won't do it at all – it's boring.'

Clive laughed and said, 'Right, we can start in the morning. What hours do you want to do?' 'I'm going to do that light jog in the morning, and then I'm going to come here to the gym,'

I told him. 'I'm going to do my weights and the fitness with yourself, and I'm going to go swimming and boxing in the evenings.' He looked at me for a moment. 'That's a lot of work, James, are you sure?' I replied, 'It is, but I need to do it. I don't want to lose this fight.' 'All right then,' he said, 'but I want you to eat the right things for the next couple of weeks too. When you get here tomorrow I'm going to give you a nutritional diet that will help you. What you can eat, what you mustn't eat, that sort of thing. You'll need to get yourself some vitamins as well.'

When I jogged to the gym at eleven the following morning, Clive started me on a small workout and a basic weight-training programme. For the next fourteen days I worked hard every day, ate what Clive told me to, and when the day of the fight came round I was ready.

On the morning of the fight I was due to be picked up at eleven o'clock. As usual, when I got out of bed I had my breakfast, had a bit of a stretch, then a bit of a shadow-box out the back of the trailer, just to loosen up. As I turned to go back in the trailer I saw loads of cars coming down the lane towards the site. The word was out on the fight, and they'd all arrived more or less at the same time; about a hundred Quinns and other people wanting to know, 'Can I go with you to the fight, James?'

I knew then my way of life was changing, when I saw so many people – people I didn't go drinking with regularly, so a lot of unfamiliar faces among them – showing an interest in seeing me fight. I had taken the challenge from Jody's Joe because I'd hit his cousin with a crutch. These people were gathered not for that reason, not even to support me in the fight, not really. They were there because a Quinn McDonagh was fighting a Joyce, and they really wanted me to beat this fellow because he had that name. The feud was always simmering. I knew then that, whatever the result of the fight, it was going to go bad for someone. If I was to come home a loser the people gathered here might not take it too well; what would they do with their disappointment? If I came home a winner, then the Joyces would have a lot of unhappy people on their side. I realised from that minute that no one was going to get any good out of this, and that these feelings weren't going to be changed by the fight.

Ned Stokes, who was going to show fair play for the two of us as my referee, came and drove me down to where we were to meet Jody's Joe and arrange where the fight would take place. We got to the drive-in McDonald's where the referees had agreed to gather and Jody's Joe was already there. He stepped out of his car and it was the first time I'd seen him since the incident in Phoenix Park. Seeing him made me realise that the idea that we were about to fight when I had no animosity towards the man was absurd. 'Well, Joe,' I said. 'Well, James,' he replied. 'There's not a lot of need for this, you know,' I said, and one of the Wards who were there leaned out of his car and added, 'There's not.' Jody's Joe looked over at him and back at me, then said, 'There's not, but it has to be done.' 'OK,' I said, 'no problem. Let's get it on.' And we climbed back into our cars and set off for a spot on the back roads.

The lane we ended up on was a dead end, with high hedges and ditches on either side, so no one was likely to come walking down there. We drove to the bottom of the lane, and one of the cars was parked across the top so that no one else could follow us down there. Along with Jody's Joe and his second and his referee, and me with my two men, there were also a couple of cameramen, one from the Joyces and the other a local lad I knew from the pubs. I'd asked him to film my fight and he'd agreed.

The referees ran through the usual Marquess of Queensberry rules, only this was without the gloves, without the rounds, and without the breaks. No biting, no head-butting, and no kicking. Fight till you're finished lads, when you say you're beat you're beat, and if we see the fight going too far we're going to stop it.

I had my plan ready. I knew Jody's Joe was a good and experienced boxer, so I needed to keep him away from me as best I could. I knew I was bigger and heavier than him, so I needed to use that to my advantage. I planned to keep him at arm's length, using my left arm stuck out into his face as a way of keeping him back, and then I planned to jab him as often as I could with my right. My aim was to cut him; if I could hurt him that way, he'd start to weaken, and then it might be easier to step in and finish him off. I based that idea on a car engine: if the oil starts leaking out, the engine is going to stop working soon. Maybe a few cuts, a bit of blood spilled, and Jody's Joe would also stop. I had two plans: if my tactics going into the fight weren't working I had Plan B, but I never needed Plan B, as Plan A started working from the start.

We got into the fight and Jody's Joe let me know right away that he was a good boxer and had done a lot of boxing. He got a few nice punches on me, hurting me, but I was getting back at him, my right was getting in there, striking him, cutting him, he was starting to bleed, and I thought, this is working out just like I wanted it to. Every now and again he'd open himself up a bit and I'd get a good solid punch in. He didn't dance about much and he didn't back off from the punches, and the ones he landed on me I really noticed, so I knew this fight wasn't going to go on too long – either he'd quit, or he'd have to beat me hard. I was fairly fast in punching him, and if he moved to cover his face I'd switch to slam him in the body, throwing eight or nine punches quickly to try and stun him. If he then tried to move on me I'd step off and return to the light jabs to the face, keeping him watching what I was doing, concentrating on me so that I didn't have to worry too much about him and what he was up to.

A minute or two into the fight I had Jody's Joe backing up and I landed a good few punches on him which put him on his arse, down in a hedge. The referees had to go in and pull him out of it. I thought to myself, this is not bad: he's got ground to make up if he thinks he's going to take me. I had become that character that they – the people that challenged me, the Nevins, the Joyces – had invented, someone who hated the person in front of me. I felt anger, a fierce burning anger, I wanted to get at him, I wanted to hurt him. I drove in on him again and this time he caught me with a punch to the side of the head. My ear sang as the pain blew through it. I was going to have a cauliflower ear; it felt almost twice the size of my head. It was a massive, cracking punch, right to the head. He got me perfectly. I pushed my hand to my ear to check for blood, but there wasn't any. He hadn't cut me, the blood was throbbing in there but it wasn't coming out. I thought, the boy can punch, the boy can fucking punch.

I turned my head to one side to keep that ear away from him and struck him with another few clear punches. He started to bleed under the eye very heavily – he probably needed about ten stitches on that eye. But he swung back and found my chin open, laying into it with a beautiful little over-the-shoulder punch. It was one of the best punches I'd ever taken. It shook my whole body and I had to take a moment to recover from it – but I couldn't let him see I needed that. I wanted my second wind. Now, I couldn't let my opponent know that, so I kept just jabbing, stepping out towards him, pushing him about a bit, so he was moving away from me, and this allowed me to gather myself together a bit. He was giving me a break as well. He didn't realise that, when he was running about in front of me. I made that opportunity in the fight, and I don't think he realised that.

About ten or fifteen seconds later this thick blood clot pooled above his eye and was running down his face. When I saw him damaged like that, even though I was fighting for my people, fighting for pride, I showed a split second of remorse and said to the referees, 'Clean the man's eye. Clean his eye.'

It was probably the only time something like this had ever happened in any fight in the history of Irish bare-knuckle boxing – someone asking for his opponent to be cleaned up. Afterwards people said to me, why did you get the referees to clean his eye? You were on top then. If his eye was cut you had him. Why'd you let him get it wiped? I never hated the man. I'd say to them afterwards, I bore him no ill will. I wanted to beat him, yes, I wanted to make sure no one else would want to fight me and that meant hurting him, yes, but I never hated him.

The real story is that if Jody's Joe had carried on swinging at me – if he had followed up that punch to my jaw – he might have beaten me. And I knew it at the time, and I had to stop him from hitting me again until I was ready. So I drew attention to the blood clot above his eye because it gave me a chance to recover a bit, and I thought that he might say to the referees that he'd had enough. With his eye bleeding like that, he had the option to pull out of the fight and there would have been no shame, not when he was leaking a lot of blood. 'Joe, son, your eye is very bad,' the referee said. 'What do you want to do? I don't think you should fight any more, Joe.' But Joe replied, 'I'll fight on.' So that was it.

I had stayed fully focused and not let my concentration slip. My body had recovered from the punch, but when Jody's Joe said, let's fight on, then all pity, all love, all compassion left me. And I told the referees to move aside. 'I'm getting in.' Three or four minutes later I cut up his other eye, over the eyebrow. It disfigured him. I knew that I'd really hurt him, and I swung a right up into his face.

I hit him right on the chin and, just as I was thinking, well done, James, I felt something snap. The pain came a moment later, a stinging pain shooting right up my arm. I'd broken my right index finger. The bandages had done nothing to protect it. Immediately I thought, I could be in trouble here. This injury is only going to get worse if I hit him with that hand like that again. I can't let him see I've hurt this hand, that I can't use it, or he'll use that against me and I'll have to give in and quit the fight. I had to camouflage the fact that I'd hurt myself, and I could do that by being more concentrated, by being more angry, and by being more determined. This way, I could block out the pain.

Jody's Joe was still bleeding quite heavily, so I realised the only way I was going to win the fight was to hurry things up.

Every time he moved towards me and slung his right arm out, I'd get it tangled up in my right and then hit him hard with my left. I tried to go as fast as I could now, because he was a good fighter and I wasn't able to do much more. Some more solid hits to the body and – after about nine minutes of fighting – he gave up.

We shook hands. We've never spoken since that day. I haven't seen him more than twice since then. He was fairly badly hurt, but his body would heal. His spirit was just as badly hurt, though, and later on – not then, then I was just pleased to have won – I felt a bit sorry for him on that count. He'd got to go home and tell his people that he'd lost to me. Losing the fight left the Joyces very bitter, and I don't blame them: they lost. A few weeks later I saw Jody Joe's tape of the fight and it showed him when he was leaving the site and his family, all gathered there, sent him out with a lot of pride: 'Go on, Joe, do it for us.' Big Joe Joyce was there as well, cheering him on – and then he had to go back to all of them and face them and say, 'Look I lost. I sent for the fight, I lost.' And the Nevins – who would have taken some abuse from the Joyces for losing fights to me – would enjoy getting their own back on the Joyces and making Jody's Joe feel even worse with their sarcastic remarks and jeers.

I was buzzing from the win, felt great all the way back to Dundalk, and even the pain in my finger didn't bother me. But that evening it started to sink in that this wasn't something I could control any more. When I got back to the pub after the fight, to have a few drinks with everyone to celebrate, it wasn't like the time I'd beaten Chaps Patrick. Then he and I could have gone for a pint together. We didn't, but we could have done. That wouldn't have been possible this time; there were Quinns everywhere, Quinns I hadn't seen in years, and they were jostling and shouting and cheering and clapping me on the back. Any Joyce who came near them would have had a bad time of it. 'What about that fight, James,' they'd shout. 'Up the Quinn McDonaghs!' My father and Curly Paddy asked me how I felt, and I told them about my finger. They wanted to know more about how I'd won, so I told them, and I added, 'That was a good fight. Jody's Joe was a good boxer, and I had trained hard for it, as you know. It wasn't a long fight, it wasn't a brilliant fight, but there were some great tactics in that fight from both of us.'

I'd done my family proud, I'd done my wife and kids proud, I'd done my brothers and sisters proud, I'd done my mother proud, I'd done my name proud, but it was the start of something that I wasn't certain where it would lead me – and where it would end. I already had two fights behind me with the Nevins, and I always felt that there was another fight coming from them, that they were grooming someone to come up and challenge me. And I was only going to get older and older.

Of the fights I'd faced – against Ditsy Nevin, Chaps Patrick and Jody's Joe – this last one made the most sense to me. Ditsy had been drunk and abusive at my sister's wedding, and wanted to fight after I'd hit him. Patrick wanted to take me on because I'd beaten Ditsy – but I'd only done what the man wanted, which was to fight him. It was different with Jody's Joe: he was protecting his family. I'd hit his cousin, and I had to be challenged for that. I can understand why. But the fight wasn't something I'd chosen to do, and although I needed to feel the rage and hatred when I fought, I didn't like it afterwards. It's an awful thing to say but I could have really hurt Jody's Joe, I could have scarred him and damaged him, and even worse, I could have hit him in the head hard enough that I might have killed him: knocked a man down and killed him with a punch. And all the travellers would say, so be it, because when you're in a fair fight, hitting that person, if he hits his head on the ground it could kill him, and that's a risk both fighters have to take. Thank God it didn't happen, but I thought about the fight after everyone had left the pub and we'd gone home, and I thought about how it changed me; how I was a nice guy before it, I was a nice guy when it finished, I'd shaken his hand after the fight, but when I was in that fight, if I'd been that nice guy I would have lost. I had to learn what this aggression meant to me, and what I had to do to avoid it in my everyday life.

I went to the hospital to get my finger looked at. It turned out I'd broken a knuckle. My thick ear was with me for a while before it went down. I thought I'd got off lightly, seeing how good a boxer Jody's Joe was. I'd used my head, I'd kept him away from me, and as a result I'd done OK.

Theresa wasn't happy to see my injuries and fussed over them. It isn't easy for a traveller wife and mother to watch her man go out to fight, but the traveller's world is a man's world and that's the way it is. It's clear why it's a man's world, although that's changing too, just as the traveller's lifestyle is changing. When we were younger it was the men who did the work that earned the money, lifting scrap or laying down tarmac, picking spuds, outdoors doing heavy work in all weathers. Of course the women had it hard too but that's how the families lived then. It was changing as our jobs and lives changed and I suppose fifty years ago – thirty years ago – a man like me would have paid no attention to the worries of a woman like Theresa, but things were different now.

When Theresa was changing the bandage on my hand, a couple of days after I'd come back from hospital, she looked up from examining the yellow and black bruise. 'James, I don't want you to do this any more.' I told her I didn't want to do it either but what could I do? If I was challenged I had to take that up, I couldn't say no. She sighed. 'I don't want the boys growing up thinking it's what they're going to do, watching you fight like that.' I knew she was right about that and said so.

Our two boys were growing up and we didn't want them to get into reacting to challenges and fighting people, now that the expectations of others in the clan were on my shoulders. Things would have to be different for them, even though some things wouldn't change – like the girls my sons were starting to show an interest in, who would want to take on a traditional role, to be a nice housewife, to keep a clean house. What roles would our boys take up? They would, like most travellers, marry young: eight out of every ten young girls wanted to get married before they were twenty, have kids early, and have a happy family. The boys would be about the same age, maybe a year or two older. They'd have to provide a wife with her home and look after her, and Theresa and I didn't want them to look on what I was doing – in the fighting – as something they had to follow too.

The traveller life was still a restrictive one. Theresa had made sure the boys went to school and studied, but we never thought about what they could do after that. Settled people might think, I'll get my son in the Garda. Or he could go to college and become a solicitor or a social worker. Travellers didn't think that could happen to their sons and daughters. It's changing now; some traveller parents are thinking their children will have a different life to theirs and will follow these sorts of careers. The change was happening around Theresa and me, around JJ and Hughie, and we could see it going on.

Theresa had always been very religious and as the boys got older she was able to so some of the things she had always wanted to do, such as going abroad on pilgrimages. Like most traveller women, she'd always had a strong belief in the angels, the saints, Our Lady, St Joseph, Jesus himself. Travellers made sure they educated their kids in religion, made sure they went to Mass. This was a bit of a struggle when the boys were younger, as no kid wants to attend Mass. Three-year-olds will go to church but they'll spend their time there running around the place. I never had a problem going to Mass; it was only one hour in the week and then I could go home and watch a film or go to the pub. And when I put that hour into my life, I always felt I got a bit of luck for it and a blessing. And three or four times a year I would go to confession; I'd spend four or five minutes with the priest, seeking absolution.

I was very involved in my sons' lives, not just at home and in church. We did indulge them, gave them the things we'd not had as kids ourselves, but we brought the two of them up to respect their elders and to live decent lives. I wasn't always about, because a man's role was to be out working. I was doing whatever I could to provide for my family: I did some gardening, I had a little company running security on the doors of some nightclubs, and I made what I could buying and selling cars.

A month after my fight with Jody's Joe I received a phone call from another Joyce, Paddy 'the Lurcher' Joyce. Paddy Lurch was Big Joe Joyce's brother, and I expect Big Joe had been on to him to fight me after Jody's Joe had lost. He said, 'James Quinn, you are not the man you think you are. We know what you're like. Jody's Joe had you beat. We saw that punch he put on you, right? You get a punch like that from a man like me – I'm eighteen stone – you're going to go down. You know I can fight.'

I had beaten Jody's Joe. I thought, I can take this man. 'OK, come out,' I said. 'I'm ready for you, I'll let you know where and when.'

Why did I say that?

8

JOYCES II: THE LURCHER

After I put the phone down to Paddy Lurch, I went out of the front door of my trailer to speak to my father and brothers. We all lived close to each other – their trailers were next to mine – so when we had something to discuss it was easy to get their opinions.

Most of the time it was great having my family close by me; I'd take my cup of tea outside in the morning and there would be my mother and father and my brothers. It was a great feeling – if we were all getting on. My mother would say, 'The kettle's always on the boil in my house. Anyone's welcome to it, if they're coming in on friendly terms.' Occasionally it could get a bit much, with nieces and nephews running in and out of the place; it would seem as if there was a trail of traffic from eight in the morning, when it would be a meeting place for all the women where they'd have their fag and their cup of tea, and then later on in the evening the lads would come in and have a chat. Sometimes that got to me, even though I like visitors and talking to people, but there were times when I needed my own and my family's privacy. Living next to my family did mean, though, that I could go away for a week and leave the door open and nothing inside would be touched.

That morning I said to them, 'Look, this fighting is getting me somewhere I don't want to go. Instead of going down a road and getting a career, earning myself some money, these people are coming up and sending for me and somewhere along the line if I keep rising to their challenges I'm going to lose.' My father was happy with whatever decision I made; my brothers wanted me to fight. Curly Paddy said, 'I'll take your training with you, James. I'll spar with you and we'll get you fighting fit.'

Some other fights were arranged for the same day as mine, and one of them involved my brother Dave, who was to fight Bernie Joyce. For some reason, almost as soon as it had been arranged, that fight was called off. I don't think Dave minded; I don't suppose Bernie Joyce did either. I had already decided to take the challenge from Paddy Lurch but now I said, 'Let's do it for money, let's do it for five grand.' I rang Big Joe, part of me hoping he'd say, 'No way, fuck off then, we're not doing it for money,' because then I could tell him, 'Well, I'm not fighting as I didn't send for the fight in the first place.' But my tactic didn't work, and Big Joe didn't even hesitate before he said, 'Five grand, you say? Right, it's covered.' I had one last try, 'Well, if you can manage five grand, Joe, then let's make the bet worthwhile. The other fight's cancelled now, so as it's me out there fighting after all. Let's take the money that would have gone on that fight and put it all on me and the Lurch, right? Make it ten grand, shall we?' There was silence at the other end of the line, then a whispered conversation, and finally Big Joe's voice came back. 'Ten grand. We're agreed. But no more waiting, James Quinn. You're fighting now, that's it. When?' I wanted to be ready for this fight, so I replied, 'I'll call you about that, Joe. Give me until tomorrow morning.'

On the day the fight would be between just me and the Lurch, but before then I'd need a lot of help from my family and my trainers to make sure I was ready for it. That would take time; I would have to give the Joyces a date for the fight, but I didn't want to do that until I had my training sorted out, as I knew I would have to be at my very best if I was going to beat their man.

I went to see Clive McGuinness again. 'Look, what can we do? How long do I need?' Then with his help I worked out a schedule. We ran through some sessions in the gym so that he could assess my condition, and he said to me at the end, 'OK, James, you're out of condition. You've let yourself go from your last fight.' It was true: I'd stopped going to the gym right away, I'd gone back to normal life as I saw it, socialising, working, mixing with people, seeing my friends.

'To get you fit for the fight, James, you're going to think me a mean big bastard, getting you round those circuits quicker,' Clive told me. 'You need about sixteen weeks.' I thought about this and said, 'They're not going to give me that long. What's the best we can do?' Clive had in front of him some sheets of paper with my scores from the previous weight and fitness training sessions and, looking at these, he started outlining what I was going to have to do, and how we would have to cram that into the weeks available. 'The thing I can't offer is the boxing,' he added, but I cut in and said, pointing at the list he'd drawn up, 'I can cut this down because you're going to get me fit here with the treadmills and the weights and all that, and I'm going to have to do the swimming, the jogging, and I'm going down to Dublin to do the boxing training, and that'll mean skipping and other things as well as boxing.' Clive looked at his papers and said, 'Right, you've got to do at least twelve weeks.'

The following morning I called Big Joe. 'Joe, I've got a date for you. 'Let's fight in six months' time.' Predictably, Big Joe wasn't happy. 'James, you're taking the mickey if you think we're waiting that long. You don't want to fight, we'll just keep your money then.' This was all part of the bargaining that had to happen. I asked him when he was thinking of, and he said, 'In two to three weeks.' 'That's not going to happen, Joe. I've got things I'm doing now, I can't stop them because of the fight. How about four months?' We kept on at each other – my goal was to get those twelve weeks Clive had asked for, and in the end I managed to get Big Joe to agree to eleven weeks. We sealed the deal, rang each referee and gave them the date, which was eleven weeks from tomorrow – which was a Wednesday – and said, the fight's on. As Big Joe had threatened, we both had to agree to an important rule. If for any reason during those eleven weeks I pulled out of the fight, for any reason *whatsoever*, I would forfeit the money and it would go to the other side. The same went for Paddy Lurcher. There was no calling off the fight now.

We gathered the money together easily enough. I put in a thousand, my brothers Curly Paddy, Michael and Dave a thousand each, my father a thousand. Then we went to my uncles and my cousins and asked them if they wanted to go in with us. They would put in perhaps five hundred a head. In this way, if I lost the fight, no one would lose too much money: a few hundred, maybe a thousand. And if I won, everyone would win only twice what they put in, which, if it was only five hundred, wouldn't be a lot of money. And so the clan put together the ten thousand. A purse of ten grand sounds nice, but I knew it wouldn't amount to that much for me because once the referee had been paid, and everyone else had had their share back, I'd be looking at about five or six hundred more than I'd put in. It's a name that wins the purse – the Quinn McDonaghs, I hoped – and it's a name that loses it. I didn't actually collect the money yet; that would come later, nearer the fight. All I had to do for now was to make sure the bet was covered.

I never liked training but it had to be done. I'd rather be in the pub, as I liked socialising, meeting people. I preferred making friends to making enemies. This time I knew I had to be fitter and stronger. I didn't know too much about the Lurcher's fighting style but I knew he was more my size, and that he would be stronger than Jody's Joe – at least I thought he would be.

Every day I'd be in the gym with Clive McGuinness. I was on the diet he'd written out for me, and I swam a lot too and sparred every night. My brother Paddy became a real thorn in my side, the type of person who, if I didn't train for long enough or hard enough, would punish me for a long time. Every morning he'd be at my door at half-six. I even stopped bothering with an alarm clock because Paddy would be there, tapping on the door. He'd get me up, put me in his car, drive six or seven miles out of town, and drop me off outside Castlebellingham. 'See you in a while,' he'd say, grinning as he watched me start to jog back home along the Drogheda Road.

Then I'd head out to the gym for some sessions with Clive. I'd do a morning and an afternoon's weight training. Then in the evening, come seven o'clock, I'd climb back into Paddy's car and we'd drive down to Dublin, to the Darndale Boxing Club, and go straight into a two-hour training session. I'd spar with the bag, I'd skip with the rope, and do some more physio training. Every Saturday morning I'd miss out the gym and we'd go straight to the boxing club, where I'd spar with Paddy and some others. On Sundays I was allowed the morning off from training and then on Sunday nights – behind Paddy's back – I'd slip out to the pub, or Rooster's nightclub, and have a few pints, just to keep sane. I'd get back home about three in the morning. A few hours later Paddy would be at my door and we'd start the routine all over again, though I'd cheat with my early morning jog as I always felt a little hungover on Monday mornings.

Every morning I jogged back to the trailer, and Paddy would meet me there. But on Mondays I'd wait for him to disappear, then I'd walk down to a local garage and buy a bottle of water. There was always someone at the garage driving north, so I'd thumb a ride with them and get them to drop me off about half a mile outside Dundalk. I'd pour the water over my head to make it look like I was sweating furiously and then run the rest of the way home. It was the only way I could cope with Monday mornings, and I needed my Sunday nights to cope with the rest of the week. Paddy was never any the wiser.

The sparring I did on Saturdays was intense, because I'd brought in a good number of partners. As well as my brothers Paddy, Michael and Dave, cousins D-Boy and Cowboys Martin, and a few local lads, there were a few settled guys who were about the same height and weight as Paddy Lurcher, so that I could get a feel for where my guard would go and how I'd have to stand up to reach him – and avoid him. A fighter usually spars with just one or two partners, but I'd have sessions with all these fellows, because I needed to build up my stamina and endurance. I was trying to go for as many as fifteen or twenty three-minute rounds without the usual thirty-second breaks. My sparring partners couldn't do that, of course, so I'd have them all around the ring, maybe seven or eight of them in there at the same time. There'd be a couple in each corner watching me spar, then one would step forward as the one in the middle stepped out, so I'd keep going without stopping.

Sometimes, with the younger lads, I'd put my arms up high and let them batter away at my sides and stomach, so that I would be better prepared when the Lurch came at me. They'd hurt me, of course, but I'd take the punches. It was all part of the training; the more I was prepared, the better it was going to be for me. I was planning to use the same style and tactics that had won me my previous fights, but also, if Paddy wanted to get into some rough and tumble, if he was going to be a holder, or a swinger, or a dragger-down, rather than a boxer, I wanted to be big enough and strong enough to fuck him about, to push him off, and then catch him. I needed to be big enough, so I beefed myself up with my diet as well as with my weights, eating protein-rich foods like steak to give me as much muscle and bulk as I could sensibly get in those weeks.

As the day of the fight came closer I was happy enough with my condition. I could keep going longer than anyone because of the way I'd trained. Throughout the breaks, as the other lads rotated round, I was punching the bag. I trained myself so that I was boxing for long periods without any break at all – and lads younger and fitter than me couldn't keep up. That was when I realised that the fight wouldn't be won by the fittest man out there; it would be the man who kept going, the man who concentrated and wouldn't give in. It would be the man who focused on beating his opponent, and put everything else out of his mind until that was done. I was determined that was going to be me. I had my goal – to win my fight – and I was going to make it. And every time I thought about the kids and Theresa at home, and the cold pint in the pub, I'd get angrier and hit the bag harder.

My training became even more intensive as the big day approached. Then, on the Sunday morning before the fight, I was phoned and told it was cancelled. So I spoke to Big Joe himself and he and I agreed that the fight was off. Theresa was away that weekend and I decided I'd celebrate the end of my gruelling training by going out for a big drinking session all day Sunday. Everything was grand: the fight was cancelled.

The next morning I was lying in bed nursing my hangover when Ned Stokes phoned me. 'Paddy Lurcher's rung me,' he told me, 'and he's said that all that talk of cancelling the fight is bullshit. The fight's not off, the fight's still on for this

Wednesday.' I'd been hoodwinked into a serious drinking session that would take me a day or two to get over. 'Are you serious?' I said. 'Look, mate, I went drinking yesterday. I thought this fight was cancelled.' Ned said, 'Paddy told me not to give back any money. The ten thousand that if you don't fight on Wednesday – he gets the money.' That was their game, was it? They thought they could trick me out of the money. 'Right, Ned, tell Paddy the fight's on, OK?'

I stumbled out of bed and went and drank all the water I could take in, then headed out for a swim. I had to get the drink out of my body and be ready for the fight. I thought about their trick; they probably hadn't expected me to go and start drinking, but maybe they thought it would fuck with my head a bit if they told me it was off when it wasn't. Just as they made sure I heard that Paddy was splitting punch-bags in his training. I didn't believe that, not for one minute.

I had had a lot of drink and I wasn't feeling great, but, thank God, I had a couple of days to recover, and because I was fit, strong and young, I knew I could work the drink out of my system in time for the fight. On with the steak and eggs, on with the training, and I got myself back to being ready.

The day of the fight finally arrived, and we gave the referee our money and set off to my uncle Thomas's, where all the Quinns were gathering. The women were inside drinking tea and chatting while the men were outside gambling, and when I saw how many were gathered I did start to think, what am I doing? There were two hundred people down there, and I knew that if I allowed that to get into my thinking at the fight I ran the risk of letting this nagging feeling – that I might let those two hundred people down, that I could have done better if I'd trained harder, if I'd done this right – affect the way I fought. All these people are here because of me, I thought, while I'm only fighting to defend the Quinn name – and these are the Quinn people – so I'm here for all of them? It did disturb me a bit. My uncle Thomas could probably sense how I felt and came up to me and said quietly, 'This is your last fight, James. You're giving up after this.' He was the only one who spoke like that to me on the day, and he knew it was exactly what I needed to hear right then. It settled me right back down again.

At that moment I felt I was in the prime of my life, going out among the men playing toss and clapping me on the back. It was a nice, crisp morning, and I felt very confident about the fight. People were saying to me, 'Are you not nervous, James?' and I shrugged. 'No, I don't feel nervous.' I didn't feel too cocky, just confident with the training I'd put in, the time I'd put into it, the energy I knew I had, the plans I'd made for the fight. I was calm at that stage.

On the drive to the fight, Ned stopped the car so I could shake off the relaxed mood I was in, and prepare myself for battle. When we arrived at the site where the fight was to take place, we found that, against all the agreements we'd made on the phone, there were not only a lot of Joyces hanging about but also a whole group of Nevins. I'd already insisted that I didn't want anyone at the fight, only the referees and the cameramen and that was it. I took one look and said, 'I don't want that crowd of people at the fight,' and got back in the car.

Ditsy Nevin started mouthing off near our car, shouting, 'Get out and fucking fight, get out and fight, James. The man is there to fight you.' I said to Ned, 'Just do me a favour, will you? Please drive away. This is only making things worse. Take us down to where I fought Jody's Joe the previous time.' On the way there one of Ned's sons rang the other referee and told him where we were going; we drove to the bottom of the lane and I stripped off my shirt and started warming up.

When Paddy Lurch arrived he was already stripped off. It was the first time I'd seen him since the London days. He used to hang about the pubs, messing about and fighting. I remembered him as a bully, someone who'd go to weddings and upset everyone there by kicking the wedding cake around the place, that sort of thing. He had just been an out-and-out bully. But I never underestimated Lurch. I saw he was a little bit chubby, but I knew that there had been a lot of chubby boxers out there, big men who could fight. I knew he expected me to fight the same way I'd fought against Jody's Joe. But I hadn't seen his style of fighting at all. I had my experience, though. I had a record: four fights behind me, all on tarmac, and all wins. Paddy Lurch had a record of beating people that he knew he could beat: this gypsy, that gypsy. But I'd never seen any tapes, so I didn't know who he had beaten, or whether they were good fighters or not.

When I walked forward to where we were going to fight I could see Paddy Lurch glistening in the light. I didn't think much of it until the fight started. His tactics were to get in front of me, come on like a bulldozer, hit me and send me down to the ground. I watched and got a step in front of him, and no more than five seconds into the fight I got a hold of him. He was absolutely covered in Vaseline, smothered in the stuff. I've never seen anyone wear that much of it; it was all over his face, his ears, back of his head, his shoulders. I said to the refs, 'Hang on, he's full of fucking Vaseline,' and they both said, 'Don't you worry about it, just get on with the fight.' Fuck it, that's good enough, I decided. I'll let him have his Vaseline – it won't make any difference to me if I can't get hold of him. He obviously assumed that I would try to hold him, but in doing so he gave away his game plan, and I knew I could turn that to my advantage.

The fight started off right, according to my plan. I let him throw himself about a bit, so I could gauge his speed and his preferred type of delivery, all the while jabbing in the odd punch to remind him I was there but remembering to breathe through my nose, keep my strength there on the edge, ready to step it up any chance I got. After my other fights I'd learned how much air I needed all the time, so I kept bringing it in, filling my lungs, letting it out, feeling the air inside me, constantly getting the energy back into my body. My plan in the first two minutes was to make sure I caught him, shocked him, put him under pressure, because I knew that most fights take four or five minutes to get going while the boxers size each other up. I hadn't had to worry about that with Ditsy but with Chaps Patrick and Jody's Joe that had been the way it had gone. This time I wasn't going to let that happen: I was going to start the fight as I meant to finish it, aggressively. All the while I'd be looking to replenish my energy because I wanted to be sure I could go the distance with him if I had to.

I'd learned to watch my physical tiredness. In the last two fights I'd thought I could keep going till I needed to find a way to break. But this time – to fight differently from the way I did against Jody's Joe, so as to fool Paddy Lurch if he thought I was going to do that again – I decided to keep my energy at the top all the time, to try and finish the fight off more quickly. I knew that an even bigger enemy was mental tiredness, because it was concentration that would win me the fight. I'd seen great boxers, great lads training in the gym, who lost fights because of their lack of concentration. One second can do it. I'd seen guys out of condition who'd used their head as an advantage, instead of their body, and they'd won their fights.

I stepped in, feinted to the left, then planted a sucker right onto Paddy Lurch's chin. Down he went. I knew right away, as he struggled to get up, that I had him because I'd hit him a beautiful right to the chin. My philosophy of fighting is, when the chin gets hit, it's nature's way of telling the brain to send a message to the knees to lie down and recover. Now I'm talking bullshit probably, but that's my way of thinking and that's exactly what happens in professional fights: if a boxer gets it on the chin, his legs go. Why do his legs go? Because his brain tells him to shut down, relax, man, take a breather.

Paddy Lurch was a big man who could hit hard, so I figured that I'd be the one more likely to go down. I kept him away from me with my 'fishing pole', which worked a treat this fight, and I thought it was better to get him worried about me rather than for me to be worried about him. So I hit him and I hit him hard, the idea being to weaken him quickly and take the sting out of his punches. As early as a minute or two into the fight he went down when I hit him, and I knew from that moment where the fight was heading. It was just a matter of time.

The 'fishing pole' did its job against the Lurcher. It messed with his concentration. It took his focus away from my right and camouflaged what I was going to do. While he stared at it as I waved it in his face, I was able to send my right hard up and into him, and – remember he's a big man – he lifted a good few inches off the ground. He never saw my right coming, and that was the beginning of the end for him. He never regained his composure or his stability after that.

Halfway through the fight, bold Ditsy Nevin and his crew turned up. They'd been driving around trying to find us and they'd come across the car blocking the top of the lane. After parking their van, they were walking down towards us, jeering at me as they came closer. I heard them even though I was blocking as much out of what was going on around me as I could. Patrick McGinley turned to his son, young Patrick, and said, 'Patrick, you and Ned go up and sort that out with them.' I didn't say anything. The two of them went off a hundred yards away and, while Paddy Lurch and I jabbed away at each other, I could still hear a lot of abuse being shouted at me. Another McGinley chap turn to his dad and said, 'Paddy, there's hot words getting said down there.' But young Patrick came back and Ditsy and his lot left; they all jumped back into their van and backed out of the lane. The McGinleys did their job well that day.

In the end the fight lasted no more than about eight minutes. Afterwards some people looked at the tape and said, 'James, that fight was a mismatch. You had him down right from the start.' I knew better; Paddy Lurch was eighteen stone, he had no right to be out of condition because he'd had the same amount of time to train as I'd had, eleven weeks, and the reports I was getting back, that he was doing a lot of boxing, a lot of jogging, a lot of training, said to me that he had his fitness. He was a big, strong lad. And still I kept knocking him down.

I was certain that I'd win the fight when the Lurcher wouldn't admit defeat, either in front of the referees or on the tape, as he had so much pride, so much pride in his name that he would not admit defeat to a Quinn. It seemed he would rather get brain dead from punches than admit defeat. Now, in saying that I know I would have been the same, so I respected him for that, but the more he kept refusing to acknowledge defeat the more I wanted to hurt him because I wanted to finish him, I just wanted to get out of there. So I kept on feeling forwards with my left, and landing heavy blows on him with my right, and every time I got him he went down, but he'd get back up. I wanted him to stay down, after maybe one more, two more, three more punches. I wanted to hurt the man so that he'd stay down and never, ever come back and look and talk about me again.

I hit him again, hard, one, two – in with the left, up with the right. This last time he was wobbly on the knees, and the referees jumped in between us and said, 'Look, Paddy, you've had enough.' He pulled his arm across his nose and face and flicked the blood away. 'Did I say I was beat?' 'No, you didn't.' The referees looked at each other. Then Ned Stokes said, 'What are we going to do?' and Pat McGinley said, 'Well, I can't stop it. There's ten thousand on the fight. We've got to let them fight,' so they stood aside and let me go in again to try and finish the fight. The Lurcher stood there again in front of me. He could barely move his hands up to protect himself any more. I threw a right and he was down again. The referees said, 'Fuck this, it's over,' and pushed me away.

That was a grand feeling. I raised my arms and walked away. Ned Stokes came over with the parcel he and Patrick had been looking after and I received the purse. I handed the two referees five hundred each for their trouble, which meant I received nineteen grand. Someone handed me a phone and it was my father, and I could hear he was shouting over a group of people around him. Someone shushed them as he repeated, 'How did you do?' 'I won,' I told him, then I could hear the cheers in the background, and I thought, I'm in for a long night – there's a lot of them drinking in the pub.

'That was a good old fight, lads,' said Ned. Chaps Patrick, who was also there, shook my hand. 'Good fight, James.' 'I've finished fighting,' I said to one of the cameras following me round. 'I won't fight no one.' Patrick McGinley wanted me to stop right there, saying, 'It's what you say on the videos that makes the fights.'(I found out years later how true that was.) 'I don't want to fight at all,' I carried on, and when asked if that was an end to the feud, I said, 'I'd like to think so, but I don't think it will be, and it's sad to see that.'

I felt a bit sorry for the Lurcher after it was all done. He was wandering round while I was clutching the envelope of money and the cameras were on me – a local journalist had found us and was asking me questions too – but no one even wanted to catch his eye. Even Chaps Patrick's little boy looked away when Paddy Lurch came over. I didn't feel a need to hate him any more because I'd won and he'd lost. I think he was put up to the fight and he probably didn't want it; he certainly didn't fight like someone who'd been training for a big show-down. After I beat Jody's Joe, I think the Joyces wanted some-one to fight me and the Lurcher was chosen. I think they showed him the fight and then said to him, 'You'll be at James. Let him have his few months of glory. Let him go drinking and messing about and we'll catch him.' Then, when they sent the challenge, they wanted me to fight quickly but I wouldn't agree to that and I think that wasn't in their plan. Paddy Lurch didn't train like I did because he hadn't had the experience out on the back lanes, in the open air, like I had. He didn't know what it takes to win a street-fight.

I was driven back to the Spinning Wheel pub in Dundalk, where everyone was waiting. As the car pulled round the corner of the street, I couldn't believe what I saw. The street was packed with people, men and women and children, who'd come to celebrate the victory over the Joyces – at least, that was how they saw it. Ned stopped the car and some people ran up and dragged me out, then lifted me onto their shoulders and carried me about for a while. Everyone was cheering and whooping, and then I was put down to say something to them all. I knew that this had been the easiest of the fights I'd had since Ditsy Nevin and I wasn't thinking clearly enough to say something to stop the challenges and the jeering, so I said, 'Genuinely, he's the worst man of his name,' and that got the cheering and the shouting going all over again. We Quinn McDonaghs were united in a way I'd not seen before, at least not in those numbers, not with that roaring excitement. We'd become one, the whole lot of us, brothers, sisters, uncles, aunts, cousins, nephews, nieces, everyone – we'd all become one person, one name, for that moment. It was a great thing for them all, as well as my own family, to have a winner, to have a win behind us. Yes, it was great as the cheers rose again. It was a good feeling.

I was pushed towards the pub door like I was being pushed downriver, and the night began. There were mad celebrations, and I knew then that this fighting game wasn't going to stop. It was a good moment for me: I'd won my fight, I had a few quid divided up among the people in the pub who'd put something in, I knew I'd have a bit to spend at Christmas on Theresa and the boys, and we all had a great night.

One of the reasons why I said what I did when we were outside the pub was that the adrenalin that had seeped away from me after the fight and on the drive back had come racing back into my veins when I got the reception I did. As we stood in the pub, singing and cheering, I could feel it ebb away again. I was happy to feel it go, because I knew it was part of what I needed in me to win a fight – but it was also something I didn't like. I'd used my memory of the Lurcher's bullying of people in London, the mouthing off I'd had from him and his backers, and I'd hit him down to the ground. I'd done what I'd had to do, but now I was glad I could forget it and I no longer had any need of the anger and the ferocity. I could enjoy a drink and a chat, and that was fine. A lot of drink, a good old sing-song – that was better still.

Chaps Patrick had come back to the pub with us, of course, and he probably had a great night along with all the rest of us. He must have had a driver as he was there with us till the early hours of the following morning. I didn't think much about it, any more than I thought much about the phone call I took from Big Joe Joyce the next day. I was home having my breakfast when Big Joe rang. He'd called to congratulate me on the fight, and on the few quid I'd taken home with me. 'At the moment, James, that was the best man we had. Paddy was sent out to beat you and be the best man, that was the aim of the exercise – but that's you.'

So I was very surprised when the day after that Chaps Patrick rang me and said, 'James, I want to fight you again.' This was followed by a video he sent round where he was challenging me, being very abusive. And who should show up on this tape – bearing in mind he's not a Nevin like Chaps but a Joyce – but old Big Joe too, also being abusive towards me, saying that when Chaps Patrick beats me he's going to give me a couple of slaps round the ears as well. 'Shows the kind of guy Big Joe is,' I said to Curly Paddy, 'when he could ring me to congratulate me one day and the following day make a tape to say he's going to slap me round the head. A real Jekyll and Hyde.'

I heard that when the Lurch went back to Big Joe and his other brothers after the fight he got a lot of abuse. They fucked him about a bit and said, look, you're not one of us, you're no good, why'd you give in, why'd you give up? We thought you were better than this. Paddy, I'm sure, doesn't want my opinion, let alone my sympathy, but I did pity him when I heard this story because at the end of the day if I lost my fight and went home and my brothers verbally abused me for fighting for my clan of people and losing, I would disown them.

The sting for them all, the Joyces, the Nevins, was all the worse because the fight made the papers. After my fight with Paddy Lurch, the following day my cousin Martin, from Dundalk, came to see me and said, 'You know your fight is in the paper?' I knew there'd been someone there from the *Star*, but I was still surprised that they'd run anything about it. 'Is it embarrassing? Is it on what, page five, page six?' Martin laughed. 'It's page one, James, and pages two and three inside.' He unfolded a copy he'd tucked away, to surprise me. 'BLOOD MONEY,' read the headline on the front page, and there was a huge photograph of me leaning over Paddy Lurch. Inside was a double-page spread with more photos of the fight. '£20,000 blood money for the King of the Travellers,' it said, as if anyone had ever used those words or even thought them. None of us there had, anyway.

I was proud for my family to see our name in the paper, but only of course because I'd won. I didn't think then at all about how the Joyces felt seeing their man beaten, and all the photographs showing him down or bloodied. If I'd thought about it at all I'd have realised that this was going to be another thing they'd hold against me.

I walked into my local pub in Dundalk that night, and seven or eight copies of the *Star* lay on tables all over the pub, and when I walked in the drinkers with those papers leapt up to buy me a drink. A lot of the people loved it, it made great reading, it was a good story, and here they all were drinking with someone who was in the paper. I liked it too, I admit. But I knew that although stories like that sell papers, it was portrayed all wrong. The fight wasn't about 'blood money'; it was about family pride.

People who knew me knew I wasn't a violent person. They knew me as a socialiser, a good mixer, a good friend to them. Other people who didn't know me, looking at the photograph on the front of the newspaper, would have thought I was little better than an animal. A man with no regard for human life, trying to kill someone or injure someone, as I had done to Paddy Lurch.

For the next few days I had journalists all over me every time I went out, pushing each other to give me their numbers, saying that they'd donate interview fees to charity because I always refused to take money from them. 'Pay the money to Our Lady's Hospital in Drogheda,' I'd always tell them, and I hope they did. Of course I got a lot of crap from the Joyces, some of them ringing me, saying, 'Charity my arse. That money is going to you, you're keeping it yourself, you baldy bastard, aren't you?'

I didn't care. The fight was over, and that meant I didn't have to get up at six in the morning to go jogging. Dinnertime would come and I'd be home with the family, not driving off to Dublin to go to the boxing club. I could go and have a pint when I wanted. The pressure was off me and my family, and the pressure was off my name.

Uncle Thomas was right. That was my last fight. It was all over.

9

THE NIGHT AT THE
SPINNING WHEEL

A fight was arranged to take place in Manchester: with a Joyce, another cousin of mine. This was part of the feud, the Quinn–Joyce thing, but it was different too: I wasn't fighting the man because I'd offended his family or anything. It was a fight for money. After the fight against the Lurcher the papers had started calling me 'King of the Travellers' and although I thought it was nonsense someone decided it would be a good idea to stage a fight in England, and the winner could then claim the title as if it was official. The referee for the fight was a man called Paddy Doherty. Later on he became known in Britain because of the *Big Fat Gypsy Wedding* programme, and in September 2011 he won *Celebrity Big Brother*.

I hadn't even started training for the fight – I don't know how far negotiations about the amount of money we'd bet on it had got – when the chance for me to take part in it vanished, overnight.

About a month before the fight I was at home in Dundalk one evening, when there was a knock at the door. I recognised the man standing there: he worked at the pub where I was a regular, the Spinning Wheel in Bridge Street. He did a bit of work clearing the ashtrays, sweeping the floor, and got himself a few pints as a reward. Tonight he was obviously earning an extra pint by running this errand. 'James, there's some fellas at the pub asking for you. Will you come down and speak to them?' It was a bit late, and I'd been in bed when he'd knocked at the door, so I said, 'Do you know who they are, what they want?' He replied, 'No, James, I think they're travellers. They were asking for you, that's all I know.' Maybe if a group of travellers had shown up there it was something to do with the fight in Manchester and it might be a good idea if I went along to talk to them. 'I'll get down there and have a word with them.'

At the pub there were two or three men I knew drinking at the bar, and I said, 'Lads, I've heard there were some travellers looking for me. Do you know where they are now?'

'No, James, we don't know. Stop and have a drink.'

Then I saw someone outside starting to pull down the metal shutters over the door of the pub. There was an odd atmosphere in the place; it seemed like they were waiting for something to happen but I wasn't sure what. So I decided not to have that drink but to look around the pub for these fellows and, if I didn't find them, get out of there and go home.

THE NIGHT AT THE SPINNING WHEEL

I walked through the pub and down past the pool table. The fat barman was waddling the other way, carrying some dirty glasses. 'Who was it who was looking for me?' I asked him, and he said, 'There was a couple of fellas earlier on. They'll be back in a minute or two.'

Next to the pool table was the women's toilet and I heard some muttering coming from there – men's voices – and I thought, shit, I don't think this is a good thing, there's something I don't like here. Just as I was turning round to head back up to the bar and out of the place, the door opened and five men with balaclavas over their heads appeared. Two of them had guns in their hands and they were pointing them at me. I rocked back on my heels. What was going on? 'Lie down on the ground!' they ordered.

I shifted backwards, away from them, until I could feel the edge of the bar pressing into my back. There was no noise anywhere else in the pub; the men behind me had stopped talking.

'Jimmy Quinn, we want to talk to you outside. Come on out the back, now.' A local accent, from Dundalk, but I didn't recognise the voice.

Shit, shit, *shit*. 'No, I won't. I'm staying right here.'

The men came closer and while the ones with the guns stayed in front of me, the others came to the side and grabbed my arms. 'Outside, Jimmy, now. We've got things to talk about. Get outside.'

They started trying to pull on my arms and I pulled back from them and slipped down. At the bottom of the bar was one of those railings for drinkers to rest their feet on, and I reached out and grabbed hold of it with both hands. I knew if I went out the back with those two men with guns that I might not be coming back in again. 'No,' I shouted back. 'If you've got something to say to me, you can say it here.' This wasn't me being brave – I just knew if I did what they said and followed them, I wouldn't be safe out there. 'C'mon, what is it you want?'

'Outside – now!' The men were frustrated with me and were leaning down to yell at my face, waving the guns closer to me to show they meant business. The ones pulling at my arms gave up and started pulling on my body instead, trying to drag me away from the railing, but I'd slipped one arm right through it and with my other hand I was locked tightly onto it now. The two gunmen stepped forward and started pulling on my legs with their free hands, while shouting at me to get up, to come outside, to do as they said. When I still wouldn't let go they started kicking me, slapping me on the head, and gave me a couple of sharp taps from the handles of their guns as well. They were shouting at me. I was shouting back.

'Get up and get outside, you feckin' …'

'No, fuck off. What do you …?'

'Lads, lads, leave him now, leave him alone,' said one of the men at the bar as he stepped over to stop them. He'd clearly known who was waiting for me, and what they wanted, although I wasn't any the wiser about that.

'Fuck off, will you,' yelled one of the gunmen, and shoved him back towards the bar, away from us. With their attention drawn away from me for a moment I thought I'd try to get away, so I pulled myself up but the gunman swivelled round and without any warning shot me in the back of the leg.

The noise in that small pub was deafening.

I fell back to the floor. Everything around me closed down. There was only these men, their guns and voices, and my leg. I reached down and grabbed the place where he'd shot me. The bullet had gone into my calf. There wasn't agonising pain, not yet. It was sore right away, like something hot had gone into me, but not the kind of pain I imagined there'd be after being shot.

Then reality kicked in.

'Fuck!' The other gunman yelled. 'We've got to go.' And all of them turned and started moving quickly away to the back of the pub but, when they were about fifteen feet away, one of them turned again and aimed his gun at me.

I saw right down the barrel. It was as if I was watching a film and I'd switched the speed to slow. He shouted something – I've no idea what – and the barrel flashed. There was noise and something cracked behind me, but he'd missed me. They went out the back door and that was that.

There was silence in the pub. I looked down at my leg and the blood on my trousers, staining them red. I looked round at the shocked faces of the men standing about. 'Drink,' I said. One of them passed me a bottle of Miller. I drank it down, then threw the bottle over my head – I hoped I'd hit one of the people who'd set me up. 'More.' Another one was passed to me.

'For God's sake get an ambulance,' someone shouted. I didn't say anything to anyone there, but I pushed a hand into my pocket and pulled out my phone, then dialled home to speak to Theresa. I had another swig of beer while I waited for her to pick up. 'James?' She must have wondered why I was calling her. 'Theresa …' I said, and she interrupted, 'Where are you, by the way?' 'I'm in the Spinning Wheel and I was shot.' I don't suppose that was what she expected me to say. 'What?' 'I was shot,' I repeated. There was a sharp breath at her end and she said, 'By who?' 'I don't know,' I told her, and as I did so the Garda arrived outside the pub. She must have been able to hear their siren as she asked, 'Who's there with you now?' 'I think it's the Guards,' I said as the door opened and men in uniform came in. 'You leave home now, right? I'll speak to you later,' I added, then hung up. Theresa, I found out later, straight away picked up the boys, packed some bags, and went to stay with friends.

The paramedics came and knelt beside me and cut away the leg of my trousers above the knee, then put some pads onto the wound. My leg had gone really stiff, it had seized up, and the wound was starting to throb and with each pulse my leg grew stiffer. Now the pain which had stayed away came with every pulse, waves of it pushing through my leg, each time stronger than before, and every small movement made the pain worse.

One paramedic was talking to me but I waved the bottle above my head and said, 'Beer.' The empty bottle was swapped for a full one. Meanwhile the police had arrived and were asking me questions too. I stared up at them and shook my head. 'Don't know … they had masks on … didn't recognise any voices … don't know why.'

I was gently rolled onto a stretcher, picked up, and taken by ambulance to hospital. When I got there the paramedics ran in with me to the operating room and starting preparing me for an operation. A nurse came with the anaesthetic and said, 'Are you allergic to anything, James?' 'Only one thing I'm allergic to,' I said, 'and that's bullets,' and she laughed. They had to open my leg up to remove the bullet and repair the damage it had created. Thank God, there was no major damage to the leg, but I was left with a ten-inch scar.

When I woke up I had the chance to wonder who had done this, and why. Since the Lurcher fight I was known as someone who had money. They didn't know that it wasn't my money, and even if they did they wouldn't give a shit – they'd read in the paper that I'd won thousands of pounds and that was good enough for them. If I'd taken the time to explain that the purse was split between all those who'd invested in it, that maybe thirty people in all were entitled to that money, then perhaps they wouldn't have thought it was worth trying to shake me down for it. But they hadn't exactly left me time to outline nicely for them how the money was split. Maybe they wanted to get some of the money that was going to go on the fight in Manchester, and perhaps they thought I had all that cash already. I didn't. I never went round to all those who were putting money in and collected it that early. Or maybe they wanted to tell me that I was going to have to pay it to them when – if – I won it. Protection money, in a way. Maybe they didn't care either way, but just wanted cash and I was that weekend's equivalent of a cashpoint.

Dundalk is a border town, easy to reach from all parts of the country. All sorts of people who had access to guns – and balaclavas – operated there. The men who attacked me could have been members of any one of a number of organisations, and they could just as easily have been members of none and had hoped to profit from some simple banditry. I was no wiser on that front than the Garda.

One thing was clear, though: it wouldn't be wise for me to stay in Dundalk any longer. Theresa came to see me. Her family had come up early that morning and had taken her and the boys back to her brother's place in Finglas. We agreed that when I came out of hospital we'd find ourselves a place there somewhere.

Theresa and I have never been back to Dundalk since.

For the next two years I had a good time. I hung out in the pubs, I worked, I got us settled into a nice house in Dublin, in Dunsink Lane, and I forgot about the fights and the violence and the money.

Of course I'd had to cancel my appearance at the fight in Manchester. I thought being shot in the leg was a good enough reason not to show up, but I heard that when Paddy Doherty had said that the fight was not going ahead – 'Be reasonable, lads, the man's on crutches' – the Joyces over there said, well, then the fight's forfeit. If he doesn't show up we win, that's the way the rules work. When I heard this I thought, well, if that's how they want it, then let them claim victory. It's not as if I chose to get shot in the leg to avoid the challenge, is it? But if they lack enough class to think that, then let 'em.

I decided I wouldn't take any more challenges. Theresa was relieved when I told her. 'No more fights for me. That's it,' I said. 'If anyone sends for me I'll say I'm not fighting unless there's a decent purse on offer. No one will take that up.'

That wasn't the end of my involvement with the fair fights, though. People still came up and challenged me; and people asked me to referee their fights for them. As a referee, it was important that I was seen to be fair, so I was happy for my friend Ian Palmer – who had started to make a documentary about bare-knuckle fighting and who had filmed my fight with the Lurcher – to come and film the fights I refereed. I had to be seen to be fair to both sides in a fight and to stand by the agreed rules, because if I was seen to favour one fighter over another, then this second man's family would hold a grudge against me. And that – given that the feud with the Joyces and the Nevins never went away but still simmered beneath the surface – was the last thing I needed.

Of course being a referee had another drawback. If the law decided to stop a fight, the referees were usually the ones holding the money and standing in the middle of the crowd with the fighters. But the Guards never seemed to trouble us, even when they knew very well a fight was going on. Ian, after filming the Lurcher fight, had videoed us driving off up the lane. By then it was getting dark, and just as he'd finished he'd nearly jumped out of his skin, as – from what he thought was just an empty hedgerow behind him – someone tapped him on the shoulder.

'James, I turned round and there were half a dozen or more Garda,' Ian told me later that evening when he joined us in the pub. '"What are you doing here?" they asked. I explained that I'd been filming a meeting. Some people had had a meeting and they'd asked me to film it. They didn't say, oh yes, and who has a meeting in the middle of November in a back lane? They didn't even ask to have a look at the tape in the camera and see exactly what sort of 'meeting' it had been. "Well, go on with you now," was all they said.'

THE NIGHT AT THE SPINNING WHEEL

Ian's story made me laugh, but the truth is that the Garda probably knew only too well what had been going on there but they'd chosen to do nothing about it. They must have been walking through to make sure that the area was cleared away after we'd gone. That's the attitude the law has to the fair fights; they seem to think that as long as the fighting stays within the traveller community, then it doesn't matter to the Garda. Only if it spills out into the settled community do they get involved. Ian could have been videoing anything – gangsters or all sorts; after all, who else has a 'meeting' in a back lane like that? – and they weren't even going to check. They'd obviously watched enough from a distance to know it was 'just a bunch of travellers knocking each other's brains out' – and that didn't bother them.

The law is explicit: you cannot fight in public. It's against the law but no one that I know about has been prosecuted, nothing's been done to prevent the fair fights, and the Garda just let them go ahead. If Ian had been filming in England, his camera would have been confiscated and the tape put into evidence, the fights would have been stopped and people sent to jail. I think that's right. If there is a law, then it should be enforced. That the Garda don't bother with any of that suggests they either think it's OK for travellers to knock each other about like that, or they don't think the law applies to travellers. Somehow I don't think it's that last one.

It's not as if there wasn't much for them to chase up and police. I was getting about two challenges a year after the Lurcher fight and, once people knew I wasn't going to be doing any more fighting myself, I was then asked to referee about one fight a month. That's just in my little corner of County Louth and County Meath. Across all of Ireland, and involving all the traveller clans, as far as I know there were about two fights going on every month, maybe more.

After all that Big Joe Joyce had said to me, after all the challenges, the abuse, the goading of his own brothers and cousins, I was surprised to be asked to referee a fight between Big Joe and Aney McGinley. For both men, their fighting days should have been over long ago, but something had flared up again and the two of them decided the way to settle it was a fair fight. Big Joe and Aney were both in their mid-fifties, and if my father had come to me and said he wanted to have a fight and would I referee for him, I'd have done my best to talk him out of it. Big Joe being who he was, no one managed to persuade him that this fight was a bad idea, and his challenge had been one that Aney McGinley couldn't refuse, although I'm still not sure why he went through with it.

So on a cold autumn day I found myself driving up to a remote wood. When we turned up for the fight, I was very worried. Hundreds of people were gathered there; knowing the Joyces and the Nevins as I do, I wasn't sure meeting up for a fight in a forest was a great idea. There was one road in and one road out. I was not very confident that the day would pass easily, because there was always friction between the two clans and on the day of a fight, when there had to be a winner and a loser, and if something should happen this friction could easily spill over into something worse.

I can organise a fight well. I'd find a quiet place that wasn't overlooked and where I could safely take the two boxers, the two cameramen, and the other referee – and no one else. I thought that was the right way to do things. I'd heard of fights where the spectators had themselves become violent and one of the fellows fighting had been stabbed, which to me meant that the referee hadn't done his job. So, as a referee, one of the things I was there for was to protect the fighter I represented, to allow him to concentrate on the job he was there to do.

I looked out the car window in disbelief at what I saw now: dozens of cars lining up to turn into a quiet wood, each packed with five or even six men. How could I watch the backs of the two fighters if there was a crowd of two hundred people pressing in on my guys' backs – especially as half of those there wanted their man to kill the other man? Who was to say they wouldn't try to get involved in the fight too?

Perhaps because of that worry, I was told something when we pulled over and parked our cars on the forest drive. One of my cousins came up to me and said quietly, 'James, over here.' We walked back to his car, and, leaning against it, he said, 'We heard there was a rumour the Nevins were bringing guns today, James. Just so you know, if you need 'em, we've brought some too.' He nodded towards the boot of the car.

That's all I needed. Shit. There I was, in the middle of a forest with just one way out and that was blocked by all those cars, trying to referee a boxing match while stuck between two rival clans who hated my guts almost as much as they hated each other's guts – and now there were guns. The Nevins were acting as the other referee for the day. If they were bringing guns, it didn't sound like there was much chance of fair play. 'Look, don't do anything, OK?' I said. 'Keep them in there and don't bring them out, or show anyone, or even tell anyone else, all right?' I couldn't have been clearer.

I walked away, heading for the group gathering around the two men who were to fight, looking about me as I did so. If anyone pulled out a gun and started firing, then the crowd would scatter into the woods. At least then they'd have protection. I thought about which way I might head if everything kicked off and how fast I could get away. And to think the only thing I'd been worried about on the drive over was the thought that the Guards might come down the path to see who was there in such numbers and what they were up to.

In the middle of the crowd the two fighters were getting ready. Aney McGinley stripped off, his chest bare, while Big Joe took off his leather jacket and wore only his vest. He was bouncing about, shouting obscenities at McGinley, telling him how much damage he was going to do to him. I started spreading out the spectators to get a decent-sized space for the two men to fight in. One of the referee's jobs is to make sure that the spectators don't crowd in on the fights, as there's a chance they'll start to interfere in the fight if they do.

'All right, James?' There was Chaps Patrick and Ditsy Nevin and their whole crew. Chaps was friendly enough, but Ditsy glared at me and then looked away. I kept moving everyone back, making the circle wider, all the while making a mental note of where the people who had it in for me were standing.

Big Joe came racing out to slam McGinley in the face and nose. It was the first time I'd seen Joe fight. He was vicious and unforgiving in his punching, wildly slamming his fists into McGinley, trying to hit him anywhere he could. There was no method or technique in what he did, it was all about power and speed. Within seconds of the fight starting blood was pouring from McGinley's nose and mouth. The man was brave, though, and kept upright under Joe's onslaught, taking his punches and then pushing forward to lay in a few of his own.

The crowd flowed around the two fighters, the spectators on one side of the circle making room for them, while those opposite quickly followed the two men into the centre. I tried to shove them back, away from the middle, but the space around the fighters lessened, so when McGinley stumbled backwards he didn't hit the ground but the horde of spectators instead, who pushed him back upright.

Ian Palmer was filming the fight and he got caught up in the throng of people as they moved backwards and forwards, jostling to get a better view of what was going on. I saw a few people reach forward and slap Ian on the head to get him out of their way, but there was nothing I could do to help him as I was trying my hardest to keep everyone away from the two fighters. The atmosphere had become hostile and it was my job to keep things smooth as best I could.

Big Joe was relentless, keeping on at McGinley, and he completely had the upper hand. If the fight was won on points, it was Joe's fight from a minute in. It was not an easy match for me to referee, though, with the crowd getting so involved. Joyces reached in to lift Joe's arm above his head in triumph, because they could see their man was winning and they wanted him to glory in his triumph. But McGinley wouldn't give up, and Joe, buoyed up perhaps by the fierce support he was getting, went in for the kill – and bit McGinley in the ear.

It was horrible. There I was, trying to stop two grandfathers from disfiguring each other with their knuckles – and, in Joe's case, his teeth. I jumped in to separate them. 'No biting, Joe. You're disqualified. McGinley's the winner.'

The mob went mad with frustration. 'Call it a draw, James, call it a draw,' one man bellowed in my ears. 'No,' I said. Joe had been warned. 'The rules are the rules' – I'd already had to pull his head off McGinley earlier in the fight – 'and Joe broke 'em. He's disqualified. McGinley's fight.'

THE NIGHT AT THE SPINNING WHEEL

The people around me surged in and shoved and pushed at me. I kept my cool and kept saying loud and clear, 'Big Joe's disqualified. He's bitten McGinley and lost the fight.' It was important that I announced my decision and stuck by it. With the fight being filmed, I knew it would be watched by a lot of people, and they'd see if I was a fair referee or not. If I'd let Joe get away with what he'd done, then I'd have been seen as a poor referee. I had to disqualify him. Those were the rules and Joe knew it, and everyone watching would see that I'd stuck by the rules, even if they wouldn't know quite how difficult a decision that was then. If I didn't stick to my decision and gave in to the crowd, I would never get another job as a referee and I'd never be respected again.

The other referee – one of the Nevins – wanted me to declare the fight a draw. 'We've got to stick by the Marquess of Queensberry rules,' I told him, poking him in the chest, 'otherwise we're a fucking joke. We'd be an embarrassment to the people watching this fight.' Besides, I had a responsibility to Aney McGinley as his referee. I wouldn't have wanted him to go back to his site and show his people he'd had his ears bitten and yet had still only drawn his fight. They knew the rules as well as anyone; they would want to see that I'd made sure there was fair play and that I'd shown that to their man. For the duration of the fight he was my responsibility, and I didn't want the day to end with another clan having decided the Quinns were not their friends.

I was also worried that if I wasn't seen to be firm and then something happened – a gun was pulled out, say – someone might say I was to blame for that. If I was clear and called the fight to an end now, maybe any further trouble could be avoided. 'A win's a win, a draw's a draw, a disqualification is a disqualification,' I said. I couldn't have been clearer but I carried on, 'This fight is going to be remembered. Two old grandfathers, two leaders of their clans who were supposed to fight fifteen years ago, fought today as men. They had big old reputations to protect, and one lost, through disqualification, and I stick to my decision.'

Shouting and jeering and cries of outrage came from all over the clearing. The only one who didn't seem dismayed at all was Big Joe. I saw him standing away from the mass, talking to – of all people – my uncle Anthony, who I knew he had a long-standing feud with. 'That was grand,' Joe was saying. 'What a fight. I feel grand.' He was beaming with delight – he'd shown everyone there that he'd still got it, he was still Big Joe, the man to be feared. The adrenalin was still coursing through him and he was too wired to care that he'd lost by biting his opponent.

When it was time for us to go, I felt relief. I'd managed to get through the day without any problems, none that would last anyway. And when I thought how easy it would have been for someone to take out a hidden gun and shoot at any of those people – they might have thought they were beating the other clan in the feud by doing so – then I was even more relieved.

One of the taunts I had to put up with whenever I came across a group of Joyces or of Nevins was what had been printed in the papers after I was shot at the Spinning Wheel. 'King of the Gypsies,' roared the front-page headline in the *Irish Mirror*; inside, I was called 'King of the Travellers.' I didn't care about this but the Nevins and the Joyces jeered at me when they had the chance – and today, in the woods, there were enough of them to jeer at me again.

There are so many clans in Ireland that it would be near impossible to be called 'the King' of them all unless I spent my whole life fighting. There are some 27,000 travellers in Ireland; that's a lot of fights. I didn't want that title, so that was the end of that as far as I was concerned. 'King of the three clans' – I'd take that one maybe, but only to annoy the Joyces and Nevins.

It did seem that even on the occasions when they fought each other, we Quinns were the greater enemy. When one of the Nevins had lost a fight to me, the Joyces would ring them up and taunt them – and they'd get it back from the Nevins if they lost a fight. The only clan left to fend for itself with no ally was the Quinns; it's always been us against one or the other. Or both of them.

10

NEVINS III: DAVEY NEVIN

I tried to put that whole life behind me by going on holiday. We went to Santa Ponsa in Majorca, out on the south-west coast, about ten miles from Magaluf. I'd never been to a place like this before. At home I was used to being told I wasn't welcome in one place because I was a traveller, while in England I was told I wasn't welcome because I was Irish. Now here I was and the promotion girls out on the streets would call out as I came past, 'Come in, have a free beer, stay the evening.' I was being welcomed into places. It came as something of a surprise to me, as I'd never experienced anything like this before, and I was very, very happy.

I was happier still the night I walked past a little bar called Flamingos, and – as with all the bars on the strip – there was a speaker on the wall, blasting out the noise from inside to entice drinkers in. All the other bars tried to persuade you to come in with music; this one had … my voice. What the hell is this? I thought.

Stepping inside, I glanced at a sign that said, 'Every Monday and Thursday at half five Irish Gypsy Bare Knuckle Boxing,' and when I looked up at the TV it was showing my fight against Paddy Lurcher. I was about to turn to my friends and say, would you look at that? when I felt a hand on my arm. 'Are you Jimmy? Jimmy Quinn?' I looked round and a fellow was smiling at me, another good start. 'This is my bar and I'd like to buy you a drink. Come and sit down.' True to his word, he did buy me a drink; he bought all the drinks for the rest of the week, because, he said, 'If you're in my bar people will want to come and see you, maybe watch the fights on TV at the same time. You can tell the people all about them. And you can have free beer for the time you're in the bar.' He looked round at my friends. 'All of you, if you're with Jimmy here.' He wanted me to sit there a few hours a day to bring in some customers. I can manage that, I thought.

People would come in, head over to the bar, look up at the screen while waiting for their drink, glance round the tables, and then do a double-take when they saw me. I became quite used to strangers coming up to our table for a chat, which I liked. I wasn't ready, though, for the moment when someone came up and said, 'James – can I have your autograph?' I didn't know where to look – my autograph? Me? Are you sure? 'I'm not a celebrity, you know,' I'd tell them, but they were happy to get me to sign a piece of paper or a shirt or something. I'd always said I never knew where this fight game was going to take me. Well, on this holiday I started to find out. What a holiday that was, being recognised, and being given free drinks – I'd no idea that could happen to someone like me. I'd never even had a holiday before, so this experience was a special one for me.

When I came back home to Dublin it didn't take long for me to be brought back down to earth. In 2002 I had a message to call Martin 'Elvis' McDonagh, a cousin of mine married to Ditsy Nevin's sister. I rang him and he said, 'James, did you have a good time now?' Before I had a chance to reply he went on, 'I've been speaking to my wife's nephew, Davey, and he says he wants to fight you.'

'What? Why would he want to do that?' I asked.

'He's Ditsy's son, James. It's on account of his father. He's been brought up to want to fight you ever since you knocked his father down.' He added, 'Common sense, James. You beat his father, and he wants to fight you for it.' I suppose it would have been a great story for Davey to tell his grandkids; that he grew up and beat the man that beat his father, that would have been a story to tell.

All those years ago when I'd fought Ditsy I'd never wanted the fight, I'd never looked for it. I'd fought him because he'd wanted it both times and now I was being made to fight again, and for nothing that I had anything to do with. Every time I accepted a challenge I hoped it would be my last fight, the last time I'd have to punch myself in training, the last time I would put my mother, my father, my wife and kids and brothers and sisters through it.

'I have to do this, do I, Martin?' 'You do, James, you do.' 'All right, but there's one condition. He wants to fight me, he's challenged me, I'm not the one who wanted this fight, so I'll only fight him if we can agree on this: I want to fight for money. I will only fight him if there's some money on the table and it's got to be a lot of money for me to want to fight him now.'

In the end, once I got talking to the Nevins myself, we agreed on a purse. Both families would put in £30,000, which meant that the winner would walk away with £60,000. As soon as that amount was agreed I started thinking about winning £60,000. I never thought, my share of that £30,000 will come in handy; I always thought of it as the combined amount, the full £60,000, because I knew that if I needed to motivate myself through training – which I would do – I'd need to think it was worthwhile. Sixty thousand was good motivation for me.

It was easy for us to raise the £30,000 from our side. There was a lot more interest in the fights now than there had been, probably because more people had seen me fighting on the tapes, and maybe those people thought they could make a little bit of money out of me. This time a number of them approached us to put their money in – something that hadn't happened before. I was pleased they were convinced I could win. Here I was, in my thirties, and here was this lad – a big lad he was, too – of only 23 or 24. Not only that, but he'd been raised to fight me. Davey himself told me that one day when he rang to tell me I was going to lose the fight.

'You know what, James,' he said. 'You know you're losing this fight.' I replied, 'Oh yes, why's that?' and he said, 'You're not as good as people think.' 'That's right, is it, Davey? Well, we'll see on the day, won't we?' I was going to hang up but he continued, 'I can fight for two hours. I'm going to fight you for two hours. I'm sparring for two hours every day.' 'That's brilliant,' I said, 'because I've been training to fight you for two and a half hours a day,' though the truth was I was probably doing no more than twenty minutes here or half an hour there. 'I hope you are,' Davey went on, 'because I'm genuinely training two hours, sparring two hours a day, especially to beat your head.' 'Davey, that's good,' I said. 'That's good enough.'

I put the phone down and went to the door. 'Paddy! Paddy!' I called. Curly Paddy was outside talking to our father. He came over to see what I wanted. I told him what Davey had just said. 'I'd better get my training right here,' I said to him. 'There's a lot of money at stake and I'm not prepared to lose that. What does he mean, sparring for two hours? Who can do that?' I knew Paddy would jump into my shoes to take this fight if he could, but it was my fight and the only thing he could do for me was to help me through the training. First we discussed what sort of a fight Davey would give me. It seemed, unless he was trying to fool me, that he was planning on doing what I'd have done in his shoes, that is, rely on his youthful stamina, try and tire me out, and wait for his chance to knock me down once I had no energy left. Paddy agreed, so we decided I'd need to be fit and ready for a long drawn-out battle with him.

I joined Steve Collins's gym in Cable Street in Dublin. Steve Collins was the WBO Middleweight and Super Middleweight World Champion. He had two guys there, John O'Brian and Gareth Mills, and they were the ones who helped me through the whole thing. They managed my programme, oversaw the sparring and the training, boxed with me as well, and got me ready.

Going back out on the road to jog was really hard at first. I felt trapped by something I had no control over when I realised I was having to run again, and I hated that. This time, though, I knew I had to do more than just be strong. I wasn't as fast as I had been when I was younger, so I had to make sure I could last the distance with Davey, and that meant I had to be fit to fight for minute after minute, hour after hour, to be certain I could take him.

Sparring with Paddy was the worst because he was the best sparring partner I had. He never gave up. He was like an Irish

NEVINS III: DAVEY NEVIN

Roberto Durán: he would come at me and he'd keep going. My other sparring partners would jab and feint away, but Paddy would burrow into me and wouldn't let go as he slammed punch after punch into me. He was a bulldog and he'd push me into a corner and he wouldn't stop. To get him to back off I'd have to stick out a leg and trip him over, and even then he'd still swipe at me so we'd end up wrestling on the ground. I was very glad to have him on my side; he was determined that I would win the fight, not just because I was his brother, but because I was a Quinn.

I made sure I got a lot of great help from the right people, because I knew that I had to win this fight, because if I should lose it, that was it for me. If Davey Nevin, or indeed any of the Nevins or the Joyces, managed to beat me, I was never going to get another challenge again. I understood that – I wouldn't have offered a rematch to a loser. Chaps Patrick was always asking me to fight him again and I never would, so I could hardly expect a rematch from any one of them if I'd lost. I could have walked right up to their door and asked them ten times, but not one of them would ever have fought me, and the Quinn McDonagh name would be rubbished by them. Paddy and I knew this wasn't something we could let happen.

The Nevins seemed to think they were going to win this one, with young Davey challenging. My phone would ring at two or three in the morning, I'd pick up, and there'd be some drunk Nevin at the other end: 'James, ya baldy bollocks, you. Davey's gonna get you …' and I'd hang up. I couldn't get rid of the phone number, either: I had to hang onto the SIM card until the fight was over, as I needed to have a number Davey could ring me on if there was any aspect of the fight we needed to discuss in advance. I'd switch my phone off before going to bed, but then it would ring at eight in the morning and the same taunts would be shouted at me. 'Davey's gonna kill you, ya baldy bollocks. James Quinn, he's going to prove you're not as good as you think you are.' Sometimes I'd listen patiently and then try to get a discussion going. I thought if I spoke normally maybe one of them would stop calling me, seeing that their jibes had no effect on me. I knew what their game was: they wanted to put me off as much as they could. They thought the calls were getting to me, but they weren't; really, they never bothered me. If anything, the aggravation made me more determined to take this fellow's head from his shoulders.

My training went as it had before, with my usual secret breaks on a Sunday night. Without those visits to the pub for a few – and I did try to keep it to a few – pints, I wouldn't have bothered with the whole thing, I'd have given up. The one thing I did differently this time was to spar in the open air. I wanted to get used to fighting outdoors; it was no good getting used to the smell of the boxing club and the confined space of the ring. I needed to be outdoors, fighting on an uneven surface, keeping my balance on wet ground and making sure my muscles didn't tighten up in the cooler air. Paddy and I sparred down back lanes that were closed off, in clearings surrounded by high trees, in disused sites that had a rough gravel covering on the ground. My previous fights had taken place at the end of the year, when it was dank and cool, but this time we were fighting just as summer was starting, and the sky was brighter and the air warmer. I really came to enjoy the sparring sessions outdoors, and as the day of the fight grew closer I realised I was almost going to miss these times with Paddy and my other brothers.

On the morning of the fight there was the usual gathering outside my home, but the occasion was different for me this time because, just as we were getting in the car to set off, my son Hughie ran up to me. There was a lot of clapping and cheering going on, so I had to lean right down to hear what he had to say. Hughie was only eight but he knew what I was heading off to do and as I bent down I heard him say, 'Knock his block off, Daddy!' This wasn't his only involvement. When we were in the car driving to the fight Paddy started putting my bandages on. Hughie had washed them for me the night before; he'd gone into my bag and fished them out to wash them himself. When he'd cleaned and dried the bandages, he'd brought them to me and told me that I should write on each one. 'When you put your bandages on in the morning, Daddy, this is the one for your left hand and you should write my name on it,' said Hughie. 'This one is for your right hand and you should put JJ's name on it. If in your fight you get a bit tired, then you should give him two Hughies and then one JJ. Every time you need our help, give him Hughies and JJs.'

It just goes to show how deeply ingrained in us the whole idea of fair fighting goes, that an 8-year-old boy should not only know what I was going to do, but that he thought I would be glad to have his advice and help.

The fight was scheduled to take place at eleven o'clock, but we arrived a bit late. We'd had to drive to Clonard, in County Meath, about thirty-five miles due west of Dublin. We all met at the side of the road there, but then the rest of the cars that had travelled with us were told they couldn't go any further and we'd travel on with just me, my referee, and a couple of others.

The fight took place in a farmyard. There were quite a few watching, more than I'd have liked – maybe as many as fifty in all. They were all neutrals, although I did manage to smuggle one of my cousins in, wearing a baseball cap and clutching a video camera to his face so that no one could recognise him easily. He had a phone, so he was able to call my cousins and uncles who'd had to wait behind in Clonard and relay the fight to them over the phone. He had a big job to do that afternoon.

When the fight started, I thought it would be the longest I'd ever fought, and that it might go on for as long as twenty, maybe twenty-five minutes. Davey Nevin obviously had his strategy and I guessed that it would be to wear me down, to keep away from me until I was tired out enough for him to come in and try and finish me off. I had decided to play him at his own game: I'd go the distance with him, and see if I could wear him down first. To do that, I'd decided to hold my ground in the middle and make him dance around me. I was heavier than him, by about a stone, but only an inch or so taller, so moving about too much would tire me out more quickly than him. But if he was the one doing all the moving, then he would be the one to tire faster.

The weather that day really helped me. The sun was out and I quickly positioned myself so the sun was on my back. I kept facing Davey and made sure that he was always staring into the sun. He had to waste time lifting a hand to cover his eyes, and he had to concentrate on squinting to see me clearly. I realised he hadn't had much experience of fighting outdoors – he was a strong lad, fit and powerful, but he was used to indoor training, to fighting in the ring. He'd had only one fight outdoors, which he'd won, but my guess was that he hadn't sparred outside and seen the opportunity to do to me what I was doing to him now. Those sparring sessions outside with Paddy paid off because I'd learned to use the outdoors to my advantage, wearing Davey down even though I wasn't actually doing anything. I'd learned to use every trick I could – there was no rule saying I couldn't do that, no rule saying where I had to stand. It's all down to what you can do to show your strength in that ring.

The Nevin lad was fit, though, and he kept on his toes, moving about, shifting back when I lunged forward to punch him, ducking sideways and leaning in to try to land one on me when he could. Twenty-five minutes went past, and we'd barely managed to connect more than a couple of punches each. We were both very wary of leaving ourselves open. Because the lad was a body puncher, I didn't want to raise my right only to leave my body open to his left. There's a lot of money on this fight, I was thinking. Why should I risk going in for the kill and losing this fight, so I'll just bide my time, let him make his mistake, then after another ten minutes I'll get in a couple of heavy rights, hurt him, and take him out.

I was getting in punches in here and there, wearing Davey down, breaking his spirit, breaking his will to fight. The longer the fight went on the more confident I felt, but I wasn't cocky. The crowd was restless, while the referees were getting bored and urging us on to finish it off. 'Lads, get at it, get at it.' But I didn't give a shite what the referees were saying. I wanted to win this fight, I wanted the money, I wanted the title, I didn't want Davey beating me after me beating his father. So I said to him, 'Do you know what, take your time,' letting him see I was the one in control, and if he took note of what I'd said I'd lean in and stick one on him to make that point clearer.

I made sure I kept my energy up. When he stepped back from me he was maybe two or three feet away, and I'd pull myself back while holding my stance and keeping my left arm out as a warning, and I'd glance about me. Watching us fight were travellers I hadn't seen for many years. Strangers too. I told myself, I'm not going to lose in front of that lot.

An hour into the fight we were still there, still testing each other, still sparring rather than fighting. The guy was there to run about, he wasn't there to fight. I remembered him boasting to me that he could fight for two hours and I thought, we can't fight for two hours, one of us has got to go down before then, and it certainly isn't going to be me – I'm not losing this. The trouble was, Davey Nevin never stood still. If I went to strike him, he would back-pedal away from me, and jump around. I knew what he was up to, but he didn't know how confident I felt in my strength and stamina. He may have had the edge on me fitness-wise, but I was more street-smart, and I knew how to keep myself going through the fight, which he didn't.

When the referees said, 'Lads, you've been fighting over an hour and a half now, come on,' I was surprised at how the time had seemed to fly by, because I was concentrating so hard. Along with keeping a check on what I was doing, I had been watching my opponent like a hawk; about then, I saw him starting to show his tiredness more than me. He started to breathe more heavily and I knew then that his body was sucking up his energy. I'd done my usual thing of taking air in through my nose, not letting him know I was breathing deeply, and stood off him a couple of times to let the air back into my system. Now I started putting a little bit of extra pressure on him by taking up the pace. I felt I had the energy to do this. I'd kept a little trick up my sleeve for him, something he wouldn't know from watching my fights on tape: I'd trained in the boxing club to strengthen my right-hand punch. Every session I'd taken time out to work on leading with the right, although it was a bit of a risk – especially when there was £60,000 on the table – to change my fighting style before a fight.

He couldn't handle my right hand hitting him on his head, as he hadn't planned for it and it was my strongest punch as well. It was getting at him. Then I switched back to my left and he fucked up again and didn't understand which way I was coming at him from. And I kept on coming at him, throwing punch after punch, and every time he stepped back I followed him around, putting him under pressure. Every time he'd come back at me – he was not a bad fighter – but he hadn't realised what I was up to, and every time he had to push himself to come back at me it cost him more effort. I just took two steps backwards and then went back out in front of him again. I was never away from him, I was like a bad nightmare.

After we'd been fighting for over two hours, he really started to slow down. The people who'd come to see a fight were getting tired standing about waiting for us to get stuck into each other, and the referees were getting tired. They'd started saying to us, 'Lads, stop this now, call it a draw, the fight's over,' but I wouldn't even pause in what I was doing as I barked back, 'No draw,' because I knew I was not prepared to lose. Davey Nevin had lost the fight, I could sense that now. Whenever the referees said, 'Call it a draw,' he never said anything. I didn't give him the chance to wait for me to hesitate so that he could say, yes, a draw, or even to let himself think I might be tiring – I wanted him to know I believed I was going to win. That mental edge was going to win me the fight.

I still had to be careful and at no stage did I consider going in for the kill, because one false punch could be my undoing. If I was to make a move on him, thinking he'd step back as he had done every time so far in the fight, and that one time he stepped to the side instead and I left myself open and exposed to his punches, then I'd be a fool. So, although it annoyed the referees, I still kept waiting for an opening where I could be sure he had nothing else to offer in reply.

In the end Davey did back into a corner. The referees had gradually tightened up on us – to keep us closer together and get the fight over with – so the area he could dance about in had shrunk, and he had gone and backed himself into the wall of a shed. He couldn't come out of the corner and I had him just where I'd wanted him to be, and I was ruthless. I went in on him hard and fast, with what I called my speedball, ten, fifteen punches in sequence: head, sides, stomach, left, right, jab, hook, uppercut – I threw it all in there.

The referees pulled me back and I stepped away from him. He was a mess, but he gamely came forward and put up his guard, though I could see he'd lost the will to continue. After we'd ducked about in front of each other for another ten seconds, he stopped, dropped his fists and stuck his left hand out. 'I'm done, James,' he said.

My tactics, my game plan, all that I'd learned as a street-fighter, everything had come together and it had worked. 'Lads, that's two hours forty-seven minutes,' said one of the referees. I'd hardly laid a finger on Davey Nevin for most of that time – maybe twenty punches actually connected in all, apart from that last little flurry in the corner – but it had worked. I'd given him a couple of very, very hard ones to the ribs, the body, the side of the head, and that had been enough for him.

The crowd clapped and cheered – more from relief it was over than anything else, I suspect – and shouted out that fair play had been shown to everyone. And that was the end of that.

The two of us wandered off to get a drink of water. Davey turned round as we walked and said, 'James, that's the end of this now. That's the end about me and you.' He added, 'I just wanted to fight you because of Ditsy, because you fought my father, when he was a few years older than you. I'm glad you gave me the chance to fight you.' We shook hands and he repeated, 'Me and you are finished now. We won't fight no more.' We went into the farmhouse and were given a cup of tea, and as we sat there we talked about the fight. We had a good chat and even a bit of a laugh about it.

I walked away with the £60,000. I heard later that a lot of side bets, too, had been placed on the fight. People who had bet on me winning – and people who had bet against me. I didn't know how much had been won or lost, but when I heard that so-and-so had lost money betting against me, I said, 'Fuck 'em,' because I really felt that if someone bet against me they deserved what they got – nothing. They should have known that the only way I was ever going to lose that fight was if I got knocked out, and I'd never been knocked out before.

I knew, though, that the next guy who came up and challenged me may well get me, may well knock me down, because I was going downhill. For the Lurcher fight I had been in the prime of my life, but by the time I came to fight Davey Nevin I could feel every ache and stretch during the training and I felt every knock and scrape after the fight for far longer than I had done after the last fight. So I knew then that whatever challenge I accepted after that would be stupid. Curly Paddy took me on one side and told me, 'James, you are going to get some young lad that's going to come up, he's going to be coked out of his head or bulked up on steroids, he's going to be big and strong, and he's going to catch you. And everything you have achieved for yourself and for us is going to go downhill.'

I knew that if I lost a fight, my wife, our kids, the whole family, would be taunted for the rest of their lives, so I decided I would never accept another challenge. Anyway, at my age I had no reason now to accept a challenge. I'd only be trying to hold onto something that was slipping away from me. I also knew I didn't want to go through all this – the training, the taunting, the physical hurt – all over again. I hadn't minded all that when I was in my prime, but I didn't want to do it any more.

Since then I've never accepted another challenge.

11

THE END ...

Making £60,000 for my fight against Davey Nevin may sound like a nice sum for me to pocket, but of course only some of that was mine. Most of it went to all the other family members who'd chipped in, and I ended up with no more than a few thousand. I'd only taken on the challenge because I needed the money. The last proper job I'd had was also my first, the one I'd had in London in the early nineties. Since then I'd been earning my money the way travellers always had done, doing what I could to make ends meet and hoping every now and again to have enough to do something special. The difference now was that I was no longer picking potatoes or laying tarmac on driveways; I had bigger fish to fry. Not everything I did was totally legitimate, but the people I was selling to never thought that whatever they were buying from me was legit either, so no harm done there.

It was important for me to try to get some cash in the bank. I'd look at a settled person and I'd see them coping with life. They'd complain about the pressure on them, how they were rushing around just trying to make ends meet, and I'd think, yes, I can see how that must be difficult, with your house and your car and your two foreign holidays a year. I had to think of my family and what would happen to them if I was injured – or even killed – in one of my fights. It's one thing to think about the fights as part of a feud, and that someone gets battered taking on the challenge, but they were also brutal, with real risks. I could have easily been killed every time I'd gone out to fight. I knew what it did to Theresa. I could see it on her face. That's why I insisted on the money as part of the reason to fight. It was no longer just a ruse to scare off the people who weren't really up to fighting me, but a way of putting some money aside so that if something happened to me Theresa would be taken care of.

A traveller's life is still a traditional one in many respects. A woman expects to keep a home, look after her husband and children, and the man is expected to provide for her and his family. That's the way it was for us anyway. Travellers marry for life – divorces do happen in traveller communities but it's rare. If a man's wife dies, she's supposed to go to the grave a widow, and not remarry. That's because when she dies she is expected to be buried with her husband, but if she has remarried, then where would she be buried? The same goes if her husband is in jail, doing a long sentence. She'd be expected to stand by him. Of course if she was young – only 23, 24, say – then things would be different. But it's changing now, as all aspects of traveller life are changing. In the old days, when a man died his wife would wear black for a year. A man who'd lost his wife might swear off going to the pub, and not watch TV, for a year; marks of respect like that were common, but not any more.

I had thought about this and I always hoped that if something happened to me, Theresa would remarry, if that's what she chose to do. I thought her happiness was more important than traveller traditions. I wouldn't expect my family to look down on her if she did so; there are some who think it shows disrespect to the memory of the man if a woman takes a new husband, that it puts the new man over the husband's own children in their own home, but I never felt that. I had trust in Theresa and the decisions she would have to make if things went wrong for me and I died in a fight. I knew my brothers and sisters, and my own mother and father, would support her if things came to that.

Family life is the most important thing for a traveller – and not just because we all live alongside each other. Maybe it's because we all had to rely on each other so much when we were out on the road, living in close proximity all the time. We all learned as children to respect what our parents and grandparents taught us and did for us. Travellers lay a great deal of importance on respect for the older generation and, once they've reached a stage in life where they need help and can't earn anything for themselves, how they're looked after.

If they live on their own, their family will visit all the time to make sure that they're all right and have everything they need. My mother and father lived in the trailer right next to my own home, so we didn't need to do that then, but when I moved we had to manage that differently. One of the younger grandchildren came and lived with them – there was a rota and the grandchildren took it in turns – for a week at a time, so that there was always company for my mother and father and someone to run errands for them.

Even if the older person is independent, someone will be nearby all the time to make sure they have everything they need. My granny on my mother's side – Ditsy Nevin's aunt, that's how close we all are – was on her own, after my grand-dad died, for about seventeen years. She was able to look after herself, but when she got to a certain stage her grandchildren took turns staying with her. Even when she wouldn't have anyone live with her, someone living in the same town, Mullingar, would call in to check on her as often as three or four times a day. When she got older her grandkids would stay with her, as happens in many travelling families. Doing what we know settled people do – putting their relatives in homes – is something travellers would never think of.

THE END ...

That's not to say travellers are all angels. I'm well aware that's not the case. One of the things I'm asked about often by settled people when they learn I'm a traveller is the mess they see around some traveller sites. I've already said that when I was growing up we would never leave a mess behind us on leaving a site, otherwise we'd never have been welcomed back, but since then I've seen people who've left their overnight spot in a terrible state when they've cleared off.

To the south-west of Dublin there's an area called Rathfarham, with the River Dodder running through it. There's a lovely little park, with a picnic area, where people walk their dogs and their kids play, and it's always busy in summer. About eight years ago or so a traveller family moved onto the land and settled there for a few weeks. I went to see them and I was appalled when I saw what they were doing. They'd been getting various kinds of work in the area – landscaping, felling trees, roofing, fascia-boarding, anything they could do – and the rubbish that was left when they'd finished the job they just dumped at the side of the park. They knew they were only there for a temporary period and thought that they could get away with tipping the rubbish illegally and that, when they moved on, Dublin Council would clear it. I was not pleased with them and told them so, because what they did gave those who wanted to bash travellers in the papers a reason to do so. The tipping got so bad that some of the rubbish went into the Dodder and blocked it, ruining the beauty spot. It cost the council almost £90,000, I believe, to clean out the river, once the travellers had moved off.

So some travellers ruin the situation for others, but that's just the same in the settled community – there are rotten apples in every barrel. The difference between the two communities is that travellers don't really look down on each other, and they are more forgiving of each other, except in one area: morals. Certain clans feel themselves very much above others, because of the behaviour of some of the members of those clans. They might not set up camp on certain sites if those clans are already there; or they will avoid going into some pubs if they think people from those clans are going to be there. The Joyces have a bit of a reputation here: people will not go into a pub if they think the Joyces are in there, because they think – and they're probably right – that there is likely to be a fight. A lot of travellers aren't interested in that and will stay away from those that are.

It's because of the violence that I started to break with the travelling community once I moved to Dublin. The reason I'd left Dundalk – being shot – was reason enough for me to want to leave a violent life behind. It was easy for some to say that violence followed me about, but that wasn't down to me: it was the feuds and the fighting. I never sought any of that. It was a life my wife didn't want, my sons didn't need, and it was one I started to put behind me.

It was easy to do this. I'd go to different pubs, hang around with different people. I'd avoid those places and those people that I knew would only lead me back into that life and I'd do everything I could to avoid them. When there were big get-togethers, like weddings or christenings, I'd make sure that nothing violent happened and that everything passed off peacefully. Other clans were a little wary of coming to some events with us because of the history of the feuding and the violence associated with it, but when they saw that this wasn't something I looked for or encouraged, then they'd join our celebrations happily.

There were other families that wouldn't behave like that, and for them a night out in the pub almost always ended up in a fight. I could never do that, and if I was with friends and we saw someone being threatened in the pub, we'd usually go over and say, stop that now, leave those people alone. It wasn't always that way and I can't pretend I was an angel but I never liked to see anyone being bullied.

One evening I was in a pub in Dublin called the Cappagh House. About forty of us had gathered there because my cousin Cowboys Michael was fighting Thomas Nevin and on this occasion I wasn't a referee and – obviously not being neutral – I wasn't allowed to be there at the fight itself. The women who'd come along all sat together while the men were at the bar drinking.

This was probably the first time I'd experienced what it was like to wait to hear the result of a fight. To know that, not very far away, my cousin was getting knocked about and, I hoped, winning, but not being able to do anything about it, was not something I found easy to deal with. We were all playing cards, passing the time, waiting for the result to come through, and I hadn't expected it to be so tense. Someone called from the fight, so one of us took the phone and the rest of us, along with everyone else in the pub, went quiet when he took the call, and watched to see how he reacted. When I asked the fellows with me if this was what it was like when I was fighting, they laughed and someone said, 'There was more of us then, James. It was noisier!'

Later, when the call came through that Cowboys Michael had won, the place went wild. It wasn't just the booze: the eruption came from the release of tension from us all. Glasses, full or otherwise, went up in the air or against the far wall. Men were dancing on tables, while the women scattered towards the door and the barmen pulled down the shutters and ducked behind the bar. For about ten minutes we were rampant, hollering, singing, delighted for Michael that he'd knocked his opponent down and out – with a sweet right – and it was only after about twenty minutes that the barmen opened up the place again and the women crept back in.

We were given a verbal warning not to behave like that again or the pub would call the Garda. When Cowboys Michael came in later we were careful to do our celebrating outside before we came in for another round.

THE END ...

It was certainly odd for me to experience the fight that way round. It was definitely easier for me to be active, actually doing the fighting, than sitting back waiting for news. I hadn't known it till then but I could see now what a strain it must have put on my family, waiting like that to know whether they could cheer – or would need to patch me up.

A couple of years later and I had to go through that feeling all over again, although this time it was worse because it was my own brother, Michael. At the age of 19 he had fought with the one of the Oxford Joyces, Paul Joyce, and lost. Michael wasn't doing badly in the fight but he went and bit his opponent, which meant – as when Big Joe Joyce bit Aney McGinley in the fight that I'd refereed – automatic disqualification. Nine years had gone by but that loss had always rankled with Michael. He knew he hadn't given a good account of himself out there and he wanted to make amends for having lost the fight that way. So he challenged Paul Joyce again, and although some – like me – would refuse to fight someone they'd already beaten before, Paul said yes to the fight. It was set to take place in about three months in Luton, because Michael, as the challenger, had to travel to where Paul lived.

Michael had fought outdoors, and won fights since then, but this was something that had hung over him for years. I knew why he wanted to fight: it was for his peace of mind, and to get that back he needed not just to fight Paul fairly, but to give a good account of himself. Michael would have to do a lot of training because one thing we knew about Paul was that he had grown into a hulk. He'd always been large but now he was a really big lad: about six-foot-six tall and at least twenty-three stone.

Curly Paddy and I agreed to help Michael with his training; we sparred with him, went out jogging with him, swam with him, helped him to get properly fit and ready for the fight. I told Michael about all the things I'd done that had helped me win my fights, and we trained outdoors so that he was properly prepared. We trained in the Bronx Gym in Dublin, where Michael used professional boxers as sparring partners to go some rounds with, each of them a lot taller and bigger than him so that he was ready to face Paul.

Of course we also decided there would have to be a decent purse for the fight. An amount of £20,000, £10,000 from each family, was suggested. Michael rang Paul and said, 'You know what, Paul, I don't think £20,000 is enough. I know I'm going to beat you, so let's make it £30,000 – that's £15,000 from us Quinn McDonaghs and £15,000 from you Joyces.' Paul mulled this over and came back to Michael, saying, 'If you're so sure you're going to beat me, then let's make it a real bet: £40,000, so that's £20,000 you have to put into the pot.' They went backwards and forwards like this for a while before it was finally settled: the purse would be £120,000 in total, so we'd have to find £60,000.

THE END ...

Michael himself put some money into it, a few grand. He didn't then go round asking who else wanted to cover the bet with him; instead he let people come to him. I put some money in, as did Curly Paddy and other members of the family, and by the time the job was done, Michael had a list of names and the amounts each person said they'd pay. He then nominated a cousin to hold the money for him. Sixty thousand is a lot of money for one person to hold, so it was left to the cousin to decide how to collect it and then to take it to England in readiness for the fight. This cousin probably didn't take the money himself; to foil robbers he had four friends go with him, but they were decoys and probably someone else, travelling separately, took the money across, and it reached Luton safely.

Michael, Curly Paddy and I went over to England a few days before the fight was due to take place. I didn't want Michael travelling too close to the date of the fight, because of the wear and tear of travelling and him not being on his toes keeping fit. In any case I needed to get him settled in before the day.

The morning of the fight came and I knew Michael probably felt that morning the way I felt when up against Paddy Lurcher: confident, in good condition, in the prime of life. I tried to remember that feeling in me so that I would transmit it to him. I took him on one side and told him, 'Go and fight your heart out. You can beat him. You're quicker than him, you're fast, you're strong now. You've learned how to fight him. Everything, everything you learned in the clubs, the gyms, the training, the road – put it all together. Fight for ten or twenty minutes, box well and go for it, boy. Win it. Keep to your plans. Don't let your mind drift for a moment. Don't let him in. Keep your guard up at all times. Losing is not an option for you, Michael. Do not lose this fight. You have a couple of hundred people waiting for the result and you've got to do it.'

I hadn't thought about what I was going to say until I spoke to Michael but I thought about what was on my mind when I went out to fight, and what sort of thing had helped me and what had not. The last-minute instructions by all the back-seat drivers, as I called them, telling me which way to punch, where to duck, how to move about – all of that was a distraction that I'd never needed and that I knew Michael wouldn't need. What had helped me was to feel focused, concentrating on what I knew were my strong points, my game plan, and trying to block everything else out. I tried to give Michael that, to get him concentrating on what he'd done in training, and on encouraging him by praising him. I'd always felt the pressure of fighting for my name but that pressure had helped me when it came to the fight – and maybe, I thought, it would help Michael.

Watching him climb into the car and drive off was probably the hardest thing I'd done in years. I was so used to being the one to take the family name on my shoulders, I didn't think it right that my younger brother now was carrying that. It was almost like packing my youngest son off to school, knowing it was the right thing for him, knowing that this moment had to come, but still wanting to step in and take the blows – in this case literally – myself. Michael needed to fight Paul today to conquer his own demons, but I still wanted to be there alongside him all the way. I never thought I was more capable of the fight than Michael. I knew how good a fighter he was, and how strong and powerful he was after all the training, but I had to fight back my own desire to protect him – because that's what my fights had been about, protecting our family name, and that also meant the members of my family themselves.

I knew Michael was capable and that he was completely prepared for the fight, and, most importantly, that he'd got his head right. He was in his prime – but he would need to be against Paul. The lad was enormous, and seemed twice his size, but Michael must not feel intimidated by him, or the place where they were fighting. This was alien territory to Michael, so it would feel more hostile to him than it did to Paul. The back lanes of County Meath where I had been comfortable in my fights were not like the yards and halting sites around Luton. Nothing would be familiar to Michael and he mustn't let that get to him either. It was also a hot July day, and that too would test his stamina.

I made sure not to say anything about the money. Michael didn't need someone talking to him about this, making him think about losing that money, or dream of winning it; that would only distract him.

Once the car had driven off with Michael I had to clench and unclench my fists to release the tension building up in me. I couldn't go back into the hotel and stay in my room or even sit in the bar, so we found a quiet corner outside where I could pace about and wait for news. I prayed for Michael to get help from his grandfathers in heaven.

A friend of ours, Bernie Riley, filmed the fight; he was also clutching a mobile phone on which he called me to tell me how the fight was going at the same time. Michael fought well, and halfway through he knocked Paul Joyce down to the ground. 'Paul's down!' I nearly cheered when I heard that. It might not have been the best punch ever but Michael had done what he needed to do and put him down. Everything I heard from Bernie I repeated immediately so that it could be relayed by phone to Ireland by a cousin standing next to me.

Paul got back up and he and Michael traded blows. I was happy enough with what I was hearing on the phone, but I always know that one punch could change the fight. It only needed a split second's lapse of concentration. Michael, though, kept his focus and didn't let anything break it. He got a good few punches in but as he went to hit Paul, the big lad would lean over and put his arm around the back of Michael's neck, pulling him in so that Michael couldn't reach his head to land some heavier blows. The referees kept breaking them up and shouting, 'Fair play, lads, fair play,' but it wasn't that Paul wasn't showing fair play, it was just that his size meant he almost had to do that to get at Michael himself.

After about three-quarters of an hour the referees gathered in closely around the two fighters and urged them to take the draw – 'Will you shake hands, boys?' – and they did. Everyone at the site watching, and there were dozens if not hundreds of them, clapped them. A draw was a good result, I thought. Michael had come back from losing against Paul and had more than held his own: he'd stood up to him. He'd managed to put him down on the ground. He'd not just kept the pride in his name but he'd restored pride in himself, in having held Paul to a draw this time.

'Good crack anyway,' said Michael when he was done.

I thought it could also solve a lot of the problems between the families. A draw stopped each side from feeling they'd been humiliated by the other, and maybe it would stop a young Quinn or a young Joyce from thinking, I'm going to fight to get my family's name back. No one had lost; that was a good thing that day. I was proud of Michael, as we all were. There was no talk of a rematch, nothing like that, the fight was done. Paul had been in the best shape of his life, and he didn't beat Michael. Michael was in the best shape of his life, and he didn't beat Paul. Both families were going home with their money.

It would have been very bad for us to lose our money or the Joyces to lose theirs. Money's not everything, but a lot of money is ... well, it's a lot to lose. It wouldn't have been the loss itself: it would have been the jeering – the Nevins would have been calling us up, just as they had done to the Joyces years before when I'd won my fights, and taunted them for a long time. 'The Quinn McDonaghs have your money. Go and get it back, you cowardly lot' – that sort of thing. I'm not sure we could have taken that if it had happened. The Joyces had had their revenge when I'd beaten Davey Nevin, teasing the Nevins about all that money I'd won. I'm just glad that we weren't put in that position.

Only a couple of months after that fight and the Quinns and the Joyces were all friends again. We were going to weddings together, we were going to funerals together, we were socialising together. We were talking again and we've been talking ever since. There have been no disputes whatsoever since that fight, and, please God, long may it stay that way.

Once Michael got back to the hotel, we hung around to talk to the referees but the longer we stayed there the more people started showing up. After a couple of hours there must have been about fifty people who'd turned up to see Michael. We needed to get away as there were two hundred Quinn McDonaghs waiting in a pub in Manchester to see us. A lot of them would be there not just to celebrate with us but to make sure they got their money back.

THE END ...

We drove very carefully up the M1 to the pub, called Mary D's, over on the eastern side of the city. The journey took three hours, as we never, ever went over the speed limit. A car full of Irishmen, carrying about £60,000 in cash? If the police had stopped us for speeding, and searched the car, we'd have been in so much trouble before we could explain things properly. We arrived at Mary D's and shared out the money. I expect most of it ended up spent in Manchester that weekend; it wasn't spending the money that bothered people, more the thought of losing it on a fight. Losing it to some keen police-man would have been almost as bad.

While Michael and Paul had been fighting I'd heard the sound of helicopters flying about and Bernie had said to me, 'There's a police helicopter right overhead at the moment, James.' He was concerned because he didn't want to find himself stuck on that site if the police arrived and caught them all there. We were careful anyway in our behaviour at the hotel both before and after the fight because we knew that the police in England treat the fights more seriously than they do over in Ireland. In truth, the police in Ireland don't give a shit.

A few years before I had been asked to referee a fight out in County Kildare between a couple of McDonagh lads. It was up to me to pick the location for the fight, so I, my friend Wes Kelly, and a couple of his mates drove around looking for a place to stage the fight. Could we find anywhere? No. We ended up driving out of town and just then I saw a back lane.

We went up the lane and it forked, so we took the left-hand road and down at the end of the lane found a lovely little circle, perfect for the three fights that were to take place.

The two participants followed our directions to the site, and the fights started. Two fights had finished, we were about to start the final one, and I was making sure again that the lads were clear about the rules. Then, just as I was about to tell them, 'Right, get to it, boys,' I looked up to my left. When we'd arrived I'd noticed a building just off the lane but it looked deserted and I'd thought nothing of it. This time, however, I saw what the building was: a Garda station. I knew this because there were forty police standing looking out of the windows at us.

I dropped my hands and said quietly, 'This fight's a draw.' The two lads, just about to start fighting, dropped their hands too, and looked at me, puzzled. 'That's it. No fight today. Look over there,' I told them, indicating with my head where they should look. They did, and everyone else's gaze followed. 'Let's move, everyone,' I said, and after a brief pause we all ran to our cars as fast as we could.

Not fast enough. While they'd been watching, the police had sent some other officers round to block the lane and start rounding us up. We all had to give our names, addresses and dates of birth. The Guards searched all the cars but found nothing. However, one of my friends watching the fight was a prison warden, and he said to the inspector, 'Please, I was only here because I was asked to drive. Please don't say anything about this. Don't tell the service.' When he went into work the next day he got a severe bollocking for being at a fight.

The police had not tried to stop the fights and only came down to talk to us when it was nearly over and we were leaving. If they really wanted to uphold the law, they should have come down right away. I think if we'd been fighting in a forest they wouldn't have bothered us at all. I suppose their attitude was, if the fight's going to happen in the middle of the forest, it's going to happen. If it's going to happen in a back lane somewhere, it's going to happen.

I've not been arrested for fighting or anything like that. In fact I've never been arrested at all. I've done some things that some people may not like, but they are things that have only affected people who thought they were gaining an advantage over me as much as I was taking advantage of them. DVDs for sale at the markets, for instance. Any weekend you like, if you go to any of the big markets in Dublin – or in London – there will be DVDs of the latest films on sale. When I had a stall in Dublin, there were quite a few others selling DVDs, so it was important to get an edge over your rivals by offering something that people really wanted to see. If a big Hollywood film, say, was just out in the cinemas, there'd be people coming to the market looking to buy it on DVD. That wouldn't be a problem if I had the film to sell them; but if I didn't, then by the time I did have – by the following weekend – so would all my rivals. To get round this, I had to be a little cunning. I would get a flyer from the cinema where the film was showing and get a cover for a DVD box made up from that flyer. Inside each box I'd put a blank DVD. I'd put that out on the stall and sell hundreds of them for a fiver each. The following weekend the people who'd bought the box would bring it back – 'This film you sold me's a dud, there's nothing on it. I want the film or my money back' – but by then I'd have managed to get the film and so I'd apologise, replace the blank DVD with a copy of the film, and send them on their way happy. That way I'd stolen an edge on my competitors and I'd made some money from the people who hadn't bothered to return and claim their money back. Maybe they thought, serves me right for buying a DVD in the market when I knew it was probably dodgy.

Travellers call them mace jobs – con jobs. Another one that worked for me once was when I went over to England and bought ten reconditioned plasma flatscreen TVs. This was when those TVs were selling for a couple of thousand each, maybe even more if they were top-end models. I bought some reconditioned ones, non-branded, some working OK and some not, loaded them in the van, and took them back to Ireland. I had someone remove the brand names and put on the ones that everyone wanted to buy, and I went out and rummaged through a few skips round the back of the electrical stores to find matching boxes I could put the TVs in. Then I put them back in the van and took them round to sell, all boxed up, as 'brand new, off-the-back-of-the-lorry TVs'. I might get as much as £1,000 for each TV. Of course a few of them worked, but most of them didn't work at all or gave up after only a few days. The people who'd bought them rang me on my mobile and I said, 'Oh, you'd better take that down and get it fixed. I'll tell you what, you get it fixed, let me know how much that cost, and I'll go halves with you.' They carted the TV down to the repair shop, where it would be discovered that it wasn't a Sony or a Panasonic or whatever and there was no warranty. After a few days I chucked out the SIM card and never heard from them again.

We did the same with power tools. Again we'd take a trip over to England, buy a large quantity of unbranded power tools, bring them back, and get them rebranded with all the top names. Then we would go round selling them for £150 when we'd only paid £20 for them, but they were attractive to customers because we were still selling them for less than they would have cost in the shops – if they'd really been those brands. At least these ones worked.

In the end we were doing it with any product we could, from umbrellas to curry powder, buying it cheaply in England, rebranding it, and selling it for more in Ireland. One time we thought we'd go big time into this business, and looked into buying a machine in China that could make cheap cigarettes that we could have rebranded and sold as top-quality brands in the markets and pubs. The only thing that stopped us was when we couldn't figure out how to bring a machine that big into the country without answering some difficult questions.

Travellers look at every possible angle to make some money. Of course what we were doing was illegal but the markets were full of people doing the same as us, and it wasn't just travellers having a go. If someone buys a TV out of the back of a van, off some guy he's met in the pub, does he really expect it to be legitimate?

There are other things that travellers do to make money that I can't agree with. Drugs have become a really big problem for many in the travelling community in Ireland now. It's got so bad that, if you went into a pub with travellers in it now, more of them would be taking drugs than not. I've been offered drugs – I've tried them, just to see what the fuss was about, but they're not for me and I never used them again – and I know that some travellers are in more deeply than others.

A more positive thing is that now a lot of young traveller kids are going to the boxing clubs, but not because of the feuding, but because they've seen how well people are doing at the Olympics. In the past they might have gone because their father wanted them to be a fighter, and now they're seeing that young Joyces, Wards, Nevins are fighting for their country. There's a cousin of mine whose two sons are now professional boxers; one of them is challenging for an Irish title. I hope that people will go more that way than into the

old traveller ways, and also stay away from things like drugs. It's difficult at the moment when there's so little money for anyone any more, but at least boxing offers them a route out.

But I would like the Garda to keep them fighting in the rings and not on the streets. There's only one way this is likely to happen and that's if someone is prosecuted for fighting on the streets. There is a law but it's not enforced. I'd love to see a law brought in that the boxers *and* the referees can be charged if a fight takes place. What more evidence do you need than the DVDs? The law should press charges, set an example, because some day or another someone's going to be killed. It will happen, so before it does, someone should stop it. I know this because when I was fighting I wanted to kill the people I was fighting. If I'd done that, I'd have faced a murder charge or a manslaughter charge. Why was I so foolish, risking prison, taking chances with my life, other men's lives, my wife and sons' futures? Because it's called fair fighting. It's the Queensberry Rules without the breaks. Whatever it's called, it's still illegal. My point of view has changed because the whole purpose of the fight game was to settle a dispute, or to settle a feud. And that's not happening.

What changed my mind were the scenes in Mullingar in 2008. There was a dispute about the way Cowboys Michael's fight had ended, and in the Dalton Park area maybe fifty Nevins started chucking stones and challenging the same number of Quinn McDonaghs. Someone even produced a chainsaw. It was shown live on TV, after helicopters filmed the two groups as they charged each other and hurled whatever they could find to hand into the air. I was asked by Superintendent Terry Quinn to try to mediate between the sides. I had long meetings with him and the Nevins in an effort to get the violence to stop. In the end everyone but one involved handed themselves in to the police and were given suspended prison sentences. And that worked – because if one of them commits any kind of offence, he's going to go to jail to do the time he has to serve for offences committed in the riot. This has kept the peace between them since then.

It seemed right to me to be the one doing this, but there is something funny about it too. After all those years I've spent out fighting to defend my family's name, I'm now the one that's a figurehead for a different reason: I'm the one that people come to when there's a dispute to resolve. I'm a lot happier with that situation.

It's going to be hard for me to carry that role out any more, though, as I have been driven away from Dublin after another attempt on my life. The police were no help to me then. I was witness to a couple of bare-knuckle fights, which were also watched by about twenty or thirty Garda. I'd already tried to stop the fights, I'd tried to get them to settle, but they weren't having it. I even went over to them and told them, 'Lads, look, this is going to go places you don't want it to go. Please stop that fight.' And they just stared at me and waited for me to go away. I don't know why the Garda didn't intervene to stop the fight but I believe it was because they were afraid. They were afraid that if they tried to stop the fight all the travellers watching would have piled in against them, but I don't think that would have happened then. They just stood and watched and waited for the fights to finish.

Two of the fighters were members of my family. One fight was a draw; the other one we won. The fights didn't stop the dispute with the other family, another branch of the McDonaghs, which had started when heaps of tyres were being burned illegally near my brother Paddy's house. The incidents between the two families escalated when a shotgun was pulled on Paddy and his son. The police did get involved then but things worsened when the police were actually on the site as three caravans belonging to the other family were burned down.

Other travellers stepped in to make peace, no charges were pressed over the shotgun incident, and we all shook hands. Things returned to normal and I went back to happily living in my home on a traveller's site in Coolock, next door to someone from the other family. By now we were no longer living in a trailer: I had a home on the hardstand there.

The night things came to a head was in May 2011. I was waiting up for Hughie to come home. I like to know he's back before I go round and lock up for the night, so I called him and he said, 'I'm five minutes away, Dad.' But Hughie is like his dad: wherever I am, people will call and ask when I'm getting to their place, and I'll say, 'I'm five minutes away,' but that can mean anything up to an hour. 'OK, Hughie, make it five minutes now. I want to lock up for the night,' I told him. Ten minutes later I rang him again. 'I'm just around the corner, Dad. I'm nearly there.'

Theresa and I went back to watching TV while we waited for Hughie to return. It was exactly eleven o'clock when, from our sitting room, I heard the front door creak open. I looked round. 'Who's that?' Theresa said. Hughie wouldn't creep in, so I told her, 'I'll go and see,' and went to the front door. I saw that it was slightly ajar, and peered through the two-inch gap to see what had made it open.

Standing outside my door was a man with a balaclava covering his face and a handgun pointed directly at my head.

I immediately slammed the door shut and put my foot to the base to stop it being pushed open again – the door had glass panels so I couldn't put myself right across the door else I'd be clearly visible on the other side. I held on tight to the handle and heard a voice outside. 'Fuck! We should have gone straight in!'

Theresa had come out of the sitting room as she'd heard the door slamming. I was just about to whisper urgent instructions to her when boots started thudding into our front door. I knew it wouldn't hold up for long, so I just shouted at Theresa, 'Get into Hughie's room, call the Garda, lie down by the back window – *now*.' I could tell from the noise outside that there were at least five, maybe six, men there.

As soon as Theresa was in Hughie's room she called out to tell me she was safely lying down, so I let go of the handle and ran towards the bedroom myself. Behind me what remained of our front door flew open and two shots rang out, the bullets whistling past me. Luckily both shots missed as I crashed into Hughie's room, slamming his door behind me. I wrenched the mattress from his bed and propped it against the window, so that no one could see in, and pushed the base of the bed hard up against the door.

Theresa clung to me and we waited, my head spinning as I tried to think what to do if the door crashed open. There was some banging outside in the hallway, a few muttered voices, and then it went quiet. Nobody came to the door of the bedroom. I strained to hear what was going on out there but then I heard some shouting start up outside. I listened carefully and realised it was our neighbours. 'James! James! Theresa! Are you in there? Get out now, your house is on fire!'

It's odd how time seemed to slow down and let me think clearly. I knew there was a fire outside our door but I didn't panic. I knew the door would hold against the smoke and flames for a little while, and we were right by a window so we could get out quickly. I didn't want to jump out of the window straight into the arms of the gunmen who'd come after me.

The voice of one of our neighbours came closer to the window. 'Theresa! James! Are you in there? They've gone! Get out, now!' She was brave, coming that close, I thought. 'Are you sure they've gone?' I shouted back. 'Yes, yes, they've gone. Now get out!' she replied. I yanked back the mattress and scooped Theresa up to help her out of the window, and our neighbour took care of her. I followed and then slid the window shut before running round to the front of the house to see what was happening.

It was like a war zone. The door to our home had been wrenched clean away and thrown out into the street. Smoke billowed across the front of our house and inside, in the corridor leading to our sitting room, I could see the fire. All our neighbours were outside, watching in silence as the flames tore through the building. One of them had wrapped a blanket round Theresa, who couldn't speak. Away to the right was another blaze – both Curly Paddy's trailer and his son's trailer had been set on fire, and I could see my brother limping towards me. He'd been shot in the leg. As I walked towards him, Hughie appeared on his bike, sweating and shocked. He'd been cycling home when two of the gang had popped up and yelled, 'That's him, get him,' and chased him across the park before he got away.

All I was able to rescue from the house was one suitcase of clothes between the three of us, and a box of photographs, most of which were charred and smoke-damaged. Everything else I'd ever owned went up in flames.

THE END ...

The Garda arrived, but we didn't, couldn't, tell them who'd done this. We had our suspicions but we couldn't prove anything because they'd been wearing balaclavas. If it was travellers, then they'd broken the code, because we'd agreed a peace and they'd done this against their word of honour. When I shook someone's hand after we'd had an argument, I believed it should be left at that – once peace was made, it should stay that way. If it wasn't them, then it was done with one aim only: to extort money from me. I'd had threats before now, because some gangsters considered travellers easy prey as we would rarely go to the Garda and often had ready cash. I'd always refused to pay up. Maybe this was the result of that.

I was only living on that site because the council had conned me out of my home in Dunsink Lane. I'd built my own home there in 2003 but the council decided to move travellers off that land and persuaded me to leave my home by telling me that they'd demolish it and build me a new home on the site. Several years later, I am still waiting for them to fulfil that promise, but I can't live in Dublin any more anyway: it's not safe for either me or my family. It makes no difference whether it was done with a gun or a pen: one way or another I was made homeless in Dublin. It's time for me to leave Ireland.

Epilogue

THE TRAVELLER'S LIFE

'm an Irishman and I'm proud of my nationality and my country. I'm proud of my country's history, our heritage, and of what my country has achieved. Which makes it all the harder to think that I will not be living there again; but I'm also a realist, and I know that I would not survive if I stayed there. I also think the place is going to the dogs: there's no money there any more and from what I understand there won't be much money for a long time to come.

As an Irish traveller I grew up feeling looked down upon by pretty much everyone else in society. In Spain, or over in England, I carried an Irish passport, and was treated much as they would treat anyone from Ireland: both well and badly. It was only in my own country that I felt this special stigma. I think of myself as equal to any other Irish citizen, but different. Growing up as a child and a teenager I saw at first hand how others did not think the same, and instead sidelined us travellers from the mainstream of society.

While that has changed in so many ways in Ireland today, there's still a lot of spitefulness around when it comes to dealing with the travelling community. I put that down to ignorance: people don't know what we're like, so they make things up about us rather than find out the truth. Also, a lot of people are lazy: if they see something on TV like *My Big Fat Gypsy Wedding*, they won't bother to find out who the 'gypsies' are – because they're not identified as Romanies or travellers or Irish travellers, and most of them certainly don't live like we do – but people will think that's what we're like too. Most of the travellers I know think of the programme as they would a movie. They'll get the popcorn and the Coca-Cola in and settle down to watch it, but to them it's nothing more than entertainment.

For me, two points stand out about the TV programme I've just mentioned. One is that it shows things that are nothing like our lives, things that would never be allowed to take place within an Irish traveller community. The other is how its appeal has now spread to our community and something that would never have been the case before – like the big fancy dresses and all that – is now becoming a part of our way of life.

Something that I would never expect to see in our community is an activity like the 'grabbing' at events such as weddings. 'Grabbing' is where a teenage boy will take a young girl – they're maybe 15 or 16 – and pull her outside a building or away from other people and try to get her to kiss him. Much was made in the programme about the girls' good name being challenged by these lads and their 'grabbing'. I know what I think: it's the closest thing to sexual assault I've ever seen. I was at a wedding in a hotel in the centre of Dublin and I saw a 16-year-old traveller boy try to grab a young girl, maybe a year or so younger than him, and the boy's father reached out and punched him for doing that, for trying to do something that goes against all our traditions. The lad was only trying it because he'd seen it on the TV. I can always tell when young Irish lads are copying that programme because they even put on a little English accent to go with whatever it is they're up to as well.

It's not just the boys who want to copy that show, it's the girls as well. If I go to a traveller wedding now, the chances are the bride will be in one of those huge dresses and all her bridesmaids in those luminous colours they had on the show. Only ten years ago you never saw that, but now well over half the weddings I go to will be like that. An outsider might see this and think we're the same as the TV 'gypsies', but we're not – we're copying them, but we're not them.

The other outsider view of travellers is that we're scroungers. When I was little that was always an insult hurled at us, but we weren't like that by choice: it was the way we lived, wearing hand-me-downs, getting donations of food at Christmas. All traveller families were the same – and so were many settled families too. Things were tough for lots of people who were at the bottom of the heap and had nothing, and that's not really changed that much over the years, so we are far from the only ones on the dole or seeking loans from the bank. I've read articles on the internet that call us 'scum' and 'vermin', but there is good and bad throughout society, just as there's good and bad in every family and clan and there's good and bad in every person. We're not on our own in that.

That attitude towards us has ground me down over the years and, along with the violence, it's one of the reasons why I'm leaving Ireland behind. As for the fighting, I don't want to get caught up in that world again: I'm getting too old to be able to fight some of the younger men coming up. I still get challenges, regularly. When I was in the prime of my life for fighting, I would have been able to fight them all; but now I'm getting slower and less fit. I don't want to give anyone the opportunity to take away from me in three or four minutes what I managed to make for myself over several years. That's probably what happened with Ditsy Nevin; he lost to me in a matter of minutes but it was probably more painful for him because he'd gone years without being beaten. I didn't want to lose that way, so I won't accept a challenge even from some-one I think I might beat – in case I get over-confident.

I've always had mixed feelings about the fighting. I like boxing – I have ever since I took it up – and I am proud of what I was able to achieve for my family and my family's name. But I never wanted to be out on the pedestal that the Joyces and the Nevins put me on, a target to knock down, and I don't want my sons JJ and Hughie to follow me down that road. It would be too much of a responsibility, bearing the weight of expectation of two or three hundred people, defending the Quinn McDonagh name, and although I felt I could handle it for myself I know that watching others facing it – as I had to watch Michael go out to fight – would be difficult for me. I would hate to see someone train for two or three months and then go out and lose. It never happened to me, and for that I'm glad, but if you accept the challenge you have to accept that you might lose. I watched the Joyces and Nevins and when they lost to me it was very hard for them afterwards. I'm not sure how well I'd deal with that if it happened to me and my family.

So much is changing in the lives of travellers now anyway that it's hard to see anyone returning to the days of fair fighting to settle disputes. Either things get out of hand, as they did in the riot in Mullingar, or travellers don't resort to that at all; since education changed for travellers, we now have travellers who are Garda, barristers, social workers, managers of childcare centres – it's all a great leap forward from the dark days of the 1970s and it's good to see travellers taking control of their own lives in this way.

The traveller way of life, as I see it, is dying out anyway. Living in caravans on the side of the road is a thing of the past.

Travellers were moved off the road and onto transit holding sites, which were meant to be temporary sites anyway, but during the eighties and nineties they became long-term sites. Now travellers want to move into apartments and houses, because for their families they want to have the same as everyone else: indoor plumbing providing hot and cold running water, a reliable energy supply, and all the amenities that settled people have. They want a more comfortable life than their parents. A lot of the girls still say things like, 'I'm going to get married and make my husband's dinner. I want to be a housewife, I want to have a home of my own to cook and clean. I'm going to be like the *Big Fat Gypsy Wedding* girls.' A number of them now also want jobs and careers of their own but they still want to be married by the time they're about 21. In our community, alarm bells will start ringing for a girl if she's not settled down – or about to settle down – by that age. Whereas settled people can wait till they're in their late twenties or thirties before they have to think about such things, they can get an education, get a job and a house, start to get some money of their own together before they marry – for most traveller girls, the aim is to get married and move to a home where the girl can cook and clean and let her husband earn all the money. She can't wait till she's 24 or 25 to do that, whereas a traveller lad of that age can marry an 18- or 19-year-old girl.

The traveller's life is a dying tradition and it has been left to traveller organisations like the Irish Traveller Movement,

Pavee Point, and others to try to keep our traditions going, as so many traditions are disappearing. Since I was born we've gone from living on the side of the roads into halting sites, from there to council houses, and then into rented apartments. We've gone from living apart to mingling and working with the settled people, socialising with them; now there are some travellers who won't mix socially with other travellers any more, and others still who've reached the stage where they now deny they're travellers at all. I don't understand that – I am very proud to be an Irish traveller, but I have very good friends in both the traveller and the settled communities and I would never choose one set of friends over the other.

One aspect of a traveller's life that I could never relinquish is a traveller's religion and our beliefs. I fear God, although I don't fear death because it's going to happen to everyone anyway. I just want to keep going a bit longer than other people; travellers generally have shorter lives than settled people. I like talking about religion, arguing with people about it, talking to the kids about it and educating them. I never did much at school, so I might not be able to argue and contradict people who know more than me on most things, but on religion I am certain I can because I know I'm right. I spent a lot of time at my bible studies as a teenager and it taught me not only to understand my religion but to appreciate other religions, be they Islam, Buddhism, or Hinduism. I took pleasure in telling my sons about the ten commandments, the gospels,

Revelations, the Old Testament and the New Testament. As an adult I was able to take this further by going on pilgrimages.

My family and I set off at a time when, back in Ireland, tensions were rising in Mullingar between the Nevins and the Quinns. I was ignorant of this as we travelled abroad for what became for me absolutely the greatest experience of my life. We went to Bosnia, to the town of Medjugorje, about fifteen miles from Mostar and not far from the Croatian border. Medjugorje had become an important place for pilgrimages since the Virgin Mary first appeared there in 1981.

The main part of the trip was to visit the mountain where the apparitions happened and to climb up it to where a large cross stands. In the mornings we'd go to Mass at the church of St James: Mass was said in English at eleven each morning, and Spanish and Italian masses were said throughout the day. Masses were said for other nationalities but not every day. The weather was fantastic and the place was beautiful. I felt transported by it all.

Only one thing disturbed my trip. I had taken my phone with me, and when we arrived back at the guesthouse one afternoon I fished it out of my bag and turned it on. Almost immediately it started ringing. 'James – at last,' the voice of one of my cousins came over the line when I answered it. 'I've been trying to get hold of you. There's some troubles here. We need you to come back.' He went on to tell me that trouble had broken out between the Nevins and our family back in Mullingar. Cars had been burned and bricks thrown through the windows of houses. It was getting serious, people going out on to the streets were getting hurt, and they thought it would help them if I were to come home right away.

'Let me get this straight,' I said. 'I've only just got here and you want me to come back? I've got a return booked for next week and you want me to pay for another flight, one I can't afford anyway, so that I can do what exactly?'

'James, we need you here.' That was how they saw it. I was the figurehead to them; if our family was under attack, then it was me they wanted there, to protect them or lead them or to do something – they didn't know what.

I sat on my bed and looked out at the peaceful world outside my window and thought, this is what I need right now, not that. 'No,' I told him. 'I'm not coming. I've just got here and I can't afford to come back now. I'm going to stay here and travel back next week as planned.' And I turned the phone off and didn't put it on again. No one else had their mobile with them, so they couldn't get hold of me any other way and try to persuade me to go back. There were no TVs in the guesthouse, no radios in anyone's bags, so no one could get news from home and pass it on to me, I needn't know anything of what was going on over there at all. There weren't even any English-language newspapers; we were completely cut off from the outside world. I intended this week to be one of the most peaceful weeks of my life.

While we were in Medjugorje we met up with some friends who were also over there at the same time, the Lawrences, and we took some side tours with them. Together we went into Mostar, which was about half an hour's drive away. Mostar is the city that was divided in the Balkan war in the 1990s and its famous bridge blown up. Since then the bridge has been rebuilt and the town restored to what it had been like before the fighting destroyed so much of it. It's a stunning place, and we enjoyed wandering through the streets and looking into all the little shops. On the bridge itself local boys gather, and if you pay them a few quid they'll dive down into the river. It's a big drop of over eighty feet to the water, and I wouldn't want to try it.

I walked off on my own for a while. It wasn't obvious to me at first but then I started seeing bullet holes and marks on the walls which had remained after the war, so there were always symbols of what had happened there. At first I wondered why the locals hadn't repaired them. Was it because they couldn't afford to fix them? Then I realised they wanted the holes to stay there, to remind them of what damage had been done here and to warn them against letting it happen again. I started thinking about the conflict and what had made people go to war with each other in such a beautiful place, and it was in that state of mind that I walked down towards the market place. I thought I might find someone there who could tell me if I was right, or if they were just waiting for money to be able to fix the holes.

As I came down the hill I saw a small cemetery off to my left and I thought – and I don't know why – I'll just have a little walk through there before I meet up with the others. I walked in and wandered among the graves. There must have been about two hundred of them and every single grave was for a young man not even 30 years old, all of whom had died in the war in 1992. I walked up and down past each one and realised that that's where all the people at home were heading. Young men were lying in the ground here because they couldn't agree on simple things, even in a beautiful place like this, and I thought about the young men roaming the streets of Dalton Park in Mullingar, who were all related to each other and who, if they went on as they were going, would end up in a graveyard like this.

Maybe it was the experience of the whole week, being in such a peaceful place as Medjugorje and seeing how many people had travelled there from all over Europe wanting the same things; maybe it because I was spending more time with my own thoughts than I would get the chance to do in Dublin; or maybe it was just that day in a city as beautiful as Mostar and seeing those graves among the streets and houses – young men who'd died for something that should never have happened in the first place – but I realised I'd been wrong to put the phone down on my cousin. I did have a role to play for the family, even if it wasn't the one some of them wanted. I walked back down to the market square, down these magnificent streets that had seen so much violence, to meet up with my friends. I was surprised that they couldn't see at once how I'd changed. When I got back to the hotel that evening, I rang my cousin.

'I'm going to come back and do something about this. Can you keep them quiet till I get home?' My cousin said he'd do his best. 'Just try and stop anyone from organising anything,' I told him. 'No attacks, no retaliations. Keep them from ringing round and stirring things up, OK? Another thing – can you help me find someone to talk to when I get there?' 'Who do you mean?' he asked. 'I want to talk to some senior person in the Garda, someone who can help me stop this getting worse.' 'I'll see what I can do.'

The next few days I went to Mass and drank everything in. The contrast between the world I was experiencing now and the world I'd come from, the world on the end of the phone, couldn't have been stronger. My eyes had been opened to peace and I knew that this was what I wanted to do now, not just to avoid the fights myself but to try and stop them altogether. I decided that I would take my family away from that life and lead, as much as possible, a normal life.

One day I went out to walk in the fields around the village. There were hills and olive groves and I liked getting under the trees in the mid-afternoon heat and breathing in the warm air, so different from what I knew from home. Ahead of me I saw a man coming down the hill, also walking among the trees. The heat shimmered on the ground in the distance and I had to shield my eyes, so I didn't look at him too closely. As he came closer, I stepped off the path to let him pass, and raised my face to smile at him as I did so, ready to say my one or two words of the local language – *bok*, hello, and *hvala*, thanks.

The words died in my throat and I stuttered out in surprise instead, 'Father Kelly!' In the same way the man coming past me also was shocked into saying, 'James Quinn!'

The man in front of me, in an olive grove outside Medjugorje, was the priest I'd known in Dundalk sixteen years ago. The last time I'd seen him was the same year this place was being shelled and fought over. Father Kelly was a traveller's priest; if a traveller was in the area, he was the priest they'd come to see. In Dublin it had been Father Paddy. As a traveller you always knew who was the priest who understood you more than others and who you could go to when you needed his help.

Before I could say anything else, Father Kelly asked, 'Are you here with your family? How's Theresa? And the children? What about your parents? Are they well?'

I almost laughed. It had been years since we'd seen each other and yet he remembered so much. 'There're all fine, Father, thank you. And yourself?'

He smiled back at me. 'I'm fine, James, fine. Now, what are you here for?' I told him we were on a pilgrimage, and had been to Mostar. We talked for a while about my family and what we had been up to on our trip so far. He explained he was travelling with a small party from a prayer mission in Dundalk, where he'd been living all this time, and they were passing through Medjugorje on their way to Dubrovnik. 'And somehow I've bumped into you,' he said, clapping me on the shoulder. 'Tell me what you've been up to. No more fighting, I hope?'

He'd obviously kept himself informed about what I'd been doing over the years. I explained to him that, no, I wasn't fighting any more, but that there was trouble back home that I was going to have to get back to right away, to try and sort out. 'There's people going to be hurt if they carry on like this. I can't stand by and do nothing.'

He encouraged me to be involved. He could see that I'd been changed by some of my experiences but he knew I was the same man he'd known all those years ago. 'People will listen to you, James. You should go there and try to get them to stop fighting.'

I said to him, 'Here we are in the olive grove after all these years, halfway round the world. That's amazing, isn't it?' He looked about us, at the view of the valley spreading out below. 'Look how far you've come, James. I don't mean from the village, but from home. You grew up on the back roads outside

Dundalk, you had a hard life growing up, and you've some-times taken a hard road, but look where you are now. Take that back there with you and use it to keep the peace if you can.'

We talked for a while longer before he had to go. He blessed me and went on down the hill to meet up with his party. I had looked up to him when I was younger because I could see then that he was a lovely man, and that hadn't changed. I thought it must be a sign of some sort, not to have seen him for so long and to meet him now and for him to say to me what he did. It was as if I was being shown something and he was there to show me the way, and it led away from violence.

I haven't seen him since.

Once I got back home and mediated between the families in Mullingar, I started to make my plans to leave that life behind me. The final straw was the night Theresa and I were attacked and our house burned down. It was time to leave. I'm not being cowardly, I'm not running from it, I'm not hiding from it, I'm just using my common sense in walking away from it, because it's got me nowhere good. And if I no longer live among the people that still want to feud, then I believe that I'll be out of sight and out of mind.

Theresa, my sons, JJ's wife, and our grandson – who's also called James, the name running down from my father through four generations now – and Hughie and the nice girl from an Irish family living in London that he's going to marry; we'll all move somewhere together, I hope. I'm going to start a new business and get a new life for us all. I believe it's going to be the best move for me and my family. I want to take my kids away from that environment and start something new. They're only young, they're only 19 and 24. They're two young men growing up where I grew up, in a life of violence, a life that I didn't like, a life I went into. It's now time for me to break the chain of violence and do something positive with our lives and stay out of it if I can.

I will pull away from the role of spokesman for the family. That's my choice and in the past I didn't think it was one I could make for myself. I thought I'd been elected to the post for life, I thought I had to fight, I thought I had to take all the responsibility on my shoulders, I thought I had to do all the things that people want me to do. I did not realise what I should have realised: that I had a brain in my head and tongue able to say no, I don't want to do this. I didn't want to put myself in that position but I had taken it because I thought I had to. When there's two or three hundred people standing there waiting to see what you're going to do for them and their name, then it's hard to say no – but I should have done. No one forced me to do what I did, I wasn't physically made to do it, but that expectation was too much for me to refuse back then.

It all started at my sister Mary's wedding, although the idea was in my head ever since I saw the film of Dan

Rooney fighting. Until I saw him fight I'd never known about bare-knuckle boxing and it was watching the tape that put the thought of it in my mind. I never thought, I'd love to do that; I'd love to be a bare-knuckle boxer, known for being a fighting man. I did love some things about it: I did love the feeling of winning, of going back to cheers and pats on the back and 'Well done, James!' and pints all round. But I achieved nothing with all that; all I did was risk my life. I risked killing someone else, all for that pat on the back, for the 'well dones', all for standing up for the Quinns. It should never have happened. People should think instead, walk away from trouble, walk away from feuds, walk away from violence, because it leads to a very, very bad ending. Stay away from being sent to prison and risking death. Don't risk losing a lot of your friends, splitting families, and ending your marriage.

It's not always easy, I know that. My brother Michael once fought a man in a church car park, and the Garda – who'd been called by the priest – came to tell them to move on. No officer stopped the fight or arrested anyone: they just came and broke it up because it was being fought in a place where it was too visible to the settled people. The Garda just wanted us travellers to take it away and fight somewhere no one would see. One of the cops came over and stuck his head inside Michael's car as he was being driven away. He obviously didn't see my friend Ian Palmer sitting next to me, Ian having slid a jacket over his video camera, which was still turned on. 'You couldn't fight your way out of a paper bag,' the cop said to Michael, who just replied, 'Yes, sir, you're absolutely right,' and let it go. There was no reason for the officer to insult him like that, but Michael did the right thing. The cop looked as pleased as punch with himself for saying this but we didn't laugh until we were driving off, and then we couldn't stop.

That's what people have to learn: to walk away from trouble rather than to look for it. Seeing those boys lying in their graves in Mostar had made me realise this. We can choose to stop. We can make a decision to walk away from this trouble and violence, but other people elsewhere in the world aren't so lucky and haven't got that choice. We can put our hand out, show the olive branch, and make peace. Some people in the other families don't want that – and there's some in the Quinns that don't want that either – but there are people in those three circles who would accept peace. It's the small number of rotten apples in the three groups spreading their stories, their bullshit, their lies, that keeps the feud going. They're throwing petrol on the fire.

My eyes are being opened to what is going on elsewhere in the world and how what goes on in Mullingar and Dundalk can be put into perspective. I've been able to see what else there is out there. It wasn't just the trip to Medjugorje that did that for me. I also went to New York, after being invited there by Bobby Gunn, a cruiserweight champion boxer from Canada who lived in the city. Bobby was talking to a friend in a store about this film he'd seen on YouTube of a traveller, Jimmy Quinn, in a bare-knuckle bout, and Bobby wanted to find out how to get hold of him. The man in front of him in the store turned round and said, 'Jimmy Quinn? In Dublin? He's a friend of mine.' I was at home and my mobile rang. 'Jimmy? It's John Wall, I'm in New York in a store, and I've got someone here who wants to speak to you.' And he put Bobby on.

Bobby came to Dublin and we had a great time. Later he paid for my flight to New York, and when he met me at the airport the first thing he said was, 'Are you hungry?' We drove to Madison Square Garden, where our restaurant table was right beneath the boxing ring, the ring where some of the greatest fights in the world had taken place, and the waiter brought out the biggest steak I'd ever seen. I felt like a kid at Christmas, it was a brilliant trip, and Bobby and I are now firm friends. Bobby has plans to explore the world of Irish travellers in the US – he's part-Irish himself – and wants to stage a legitimate, licensed bare-knuckle fight. I'm going to help him if I can.

Ian Palmer completed his documentary and it was released in the summer of 2011. I started travelling round with Ian, going to press screenings and to film festivals where the documentary was shown. I'd answer questions from the audience and I realised how interesting people found the story. Although I'd been trying to keep a low profile in Dublin after the attack on my home, I was happy to be there making sure that Ian's film was as widely seen as possible.

If anyone asks me about boxing, I say, get down to your local gym, learn to box, train, fight your opponent in competitions, spar with your friends, do whatever you want to do – but keep it in the ring. Get yourself a career as a boxer if you can. I won't referee any fights any more, I say, and I want them to stop. I asked my father, can you see this feud stopping? No, he replied. The next generation will find something to fight about, they always do.

Sometimes I think about how different my life would have been if I'd not been born a traveller, and I wonder: would I have had a better life? I don't think I could have had better parents than my mother and father, a better family than my sisters and brothers, my wife, and my sons. I don't think I could be any more proud of my heritage than I am. There's no doubt the life has been hard, and the challenges thrown in my path have been great ones, and sometimes I've wished it wasn't so, but to wish any more than that would be to deny what has made me. I'm a traveller through and through, and that's the end of it. I carry on doing as other travellers have done before me – I respect my religion, my community and my family. I will always do the best I can for my family, I want to be an example for them and to be a success, but I am also my own man too: I always like to say I'm in the world for a good time, not a long time.

Out there in the world, there's something else for me. I'm seeking something new now that I've left my old life in Ireland behind. I don't know what it is yet. Maybe I won't know till I've got it.

I just know it's more than I've done so far.

ACKNOWLEDGEMENTS

I would like to thank:

My wife, Theresa, and sons, James and Hughie.

My mother and father, Teresa and Jimmy Quinn McDonagh, and my brother, Dave, and sisters, Mary, Bridgie and Maggie.

My brothers, Michael Quinn McDonagh and Paddy Quinn McDonagh, for their help over the years with my training.

Humphrey Price, Ian Palmer and Teddy Leifer.

All at HarperCollins for their kindness and help with my book.

INDEX

INDEX

INDEX

INDEX

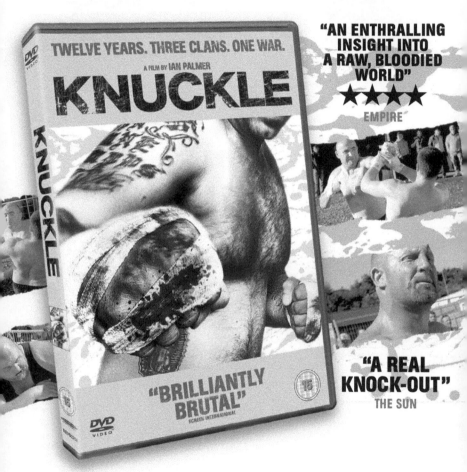

Lightning Source UK Ltd.
Milton Keynes UK
UKHW010105300620
365756UK00003B/295